the audacity
of faith

Christian Leaders
Reflect on the
Election of
BARACK OBAMA

Edited by
Marvin A. McMickle

JUDSON PRESS
PUBLISHERS SINCE 1824
VALLEY FORGE, PA

Library of Congress Cataloging-in-Publication Data

The audacity of faith: Christian leaders reflect on the election of Barack Obama/ edited by Marvin A. McMickle. —1st ed.
p. cm.
ISBN 978-0-8170-1554-1 (pbk. : alk. paper) 1. Obama, Barack. 2. Presidents—United States—Election—2008. 3. Christianity and politics—United States. 4. Race relations—Religious aspects—Christianity. 5. Reconciliation—Religious aspects—Christianity. 6. United States—Race relations. 7. African Americans—Social conditions. I. McMickle, Marvin Andrew.
E907.A83 2009
973.932092—dc22   2009011567

This book is dedicated to all the people who labored so hard and for so long to earn the right to vote for all Americans. It is dedicated to those who labored for the Fifteenth Amendment to the U.S. Constitution, which guaranteed the right to vote for African Americans, as well as to those who worked for the Nineteenth Amendment, which guaranteed the right to vote for women. It is dedicated to the young, first-time voters who saw in the presidential election of 2008 a compelling reason to go out and cast their votes. This book is also dedicated to unpaid campaign volunteers, the Obama convention delegates, the poll workers on November 4, 2008, and all the people who gathered later that evening—from the throngs who assembled in Grant Park in Chicago to those who gathered in smaller numbers in church basements and living rooms and on street corners all across America to celebrate an event that few, if any of them believed would happen in their lifetime.

This book is dedicated to the five- and ten-dollar donors to the Obama campaign who provided the resources that allowed the *audacity of hope* to shape a national chorus of *Yes, We Can*. It was the audacity of their faith that enabled a long-shot candidate to become the first African American president of the United States. This book is also dedicated to those who had the audacity to run for the presidency in earlier years: Congresswoman Shirley Chisholm (1972), the Reverend Jesse Jackson Sr. (1984 and 1988), and the Reverend Al Sharpton (2004). They know better than any other persons what it took for Barack Obama to run a national campaign and win a national election. In a very real sense, those three distinguished Americans were the seeds planted in the ground over the last thirty-six years; President Barack Obama is the harvest and the fruit of the labor of those candidates and their supporters.

CONTENTS

PART V Biblical and Theological Perspectives

ACKNOWLEDGMENTS

The process of writing a book is a very personal thing that involves long hours of solitude and the willingness to critique your own words even before your editors go to work on what you may have thought was a finished product. This book was a very different experience, because it was entirely dependent upon the contributions of so many others whose gifts and talents I have long admired. What a marvelous company of friends and colleagues has been assembled for this project. I am indebted to each and every one of them. There are not many places you can turn where Emilie Townes and Tony Campolo, Leslie Callahan and Philip Yancey, Valerie Elverton Dixon, and Dwight Hopkins, and Carolyn Ann Knight and William Willimon are bound together in the same volume. Add to that the seasoned perspectives of Gardner Taylor and J. Alfred Smith along with the fresh insights of Brad Braxton and Mitzi Smith plus a dozen more insightful contributors, and you have a very special collaboration.

Thirty-three scholars drawn from the ranks of seminary and university professors, pastors, denominational leaders, and writers have collaborated on this book. Each of them is a seasoned preacher or teacher in his or her own right, but when they came together to reflect on the biblical and theological implications of the election of President Barack Obama, they became a "great cloud of witnesses" for one of the most significant events in American history: the election of the nation's first African American president. As you might expect from the diverse group of people who have contributed to this book, the essays and sermons that have been assembled here are as rich in their diversity of opinion as they are in the depth of their content. What an honor and a privilege it was to read them as they came in from pulpits, classrooms, and writing tables from all across the country. I am the better for having been able to share this project with such an extraordinary group of Christian leaders.

This volume was inspired by *9.11.01: African American Leaders Respond to an American Tragedy*, edited by my friend Martha Simmons and published by Judson Press. It was determined that the election of Barack Obama was another historic event that warranted some biblical and theological analysis. However, unlike the earlier book, which was limited to only African American religious leaders, this book casts a wider net by gathering together views that reflect ethnic, gender, generational, and theological diversity. We attempted to secure some other contributors for this project, but their already crowded schedules and our very tight deadline for getting a book ready for publication as close to Obama's inauguration as possible prohibited some from being able to respond.

When the contributors were first contacted, they were given the option of addressing one of four possible approaches to the significance of President Obama's election:

1. In what ways does the election of Barack Obama suggest the fulfillment of the words of Dr. Martin Luther King Jr. from April 3, 1968, "We as a people will get to the Promised Land"?

2. Does the election of Barack Obama serve as evidence that the United States of America has entered into a "postracial" era?

3. What are the biblical and/or theological terms and concepts that you have used as you have reflected on an Obama presidency?

4. Is there a danger of people believing that an Obama presidency can or should accomplish things that Scripture suggests can be accomplished only by God and through the work of the church?

With those as the opening questions, this brilliant group of writers have assessed and analyzed the campaign, the election, and even the initial performance of the Obama administration with historical clarity and prophetic vigor. A full list of the contributors can be found at the end of this book, but let me say from the outset how grateful I am for their participation in this project.

As with all Judson Press releases, it goes without saying that Rebecca Irwin-Diehl was at the center of this project. She and I worked together on a possible list of contributors, but she did all the work of contacting them, answering their questions, counseling with them about issues of format and length, and, most of all, gently nudging them as the deadline for all submissions came and went. Rebecca and I have exchanged phone calls or e-mails virtually every day since the idea for this book was formally approved by Judson Press. I am as indebted to her as I am to those who contributed their sermons and essays. This is a true saying, and it is beyond contradiction: No Rebecca—no book.

I want to thank Thomas Troeger and Emilie Townes of Yale Divinity School who invited me to spend the winter semester of 2009 as a visiting professor of preaching on that distinguished faculty. This book was made possible by their hospitality as well as by the technical support provided by Robert Piscatelli and the Yale Divinity School Information Technology staff. I also want to acknowledge John Shultz, president of Ashland Theological Seminary, who was willing to release me from my duties there so I could accept the invitation from Yale. The same goes for Dale Stoffer, the academic dean at ATS who found a way to allow my teaching at Ashland to take place in our spring quarter even though Yale's winter semester overlapped that quarter by many weeks.

My wife, Peggy, deserves double recognition, because she released her husband to be away in New Haven for most days in every week from mid-January to the end of April. On top of that, she encouraged me to keep my commitment to Yale and to Judson Press even though she encountered some unexpected health challenges just as the winter semester and the editing of this book were about to begin.

Finally, I want to acknowledge the historic achievement of President Barack Obama. Like many of the contributors to this book, I was an early supporter of his candidacy, and that support extended to my serving as an Obama delegate to the Democratic National Convention in Denver, where Obama clinched the nomination and delivered a stirring address at INVESCO Field before a crowd of more than 80,000 people. Without his willingness to demonstrate the *audacity of hope* there would have been no need or opportunity for this book on the *audacity of faith*.

INTRODUCTION

From the very moment the ink dried on the parchment document we call the Declaration of Independence, the United States of America has lived with one large piece of unfinished business. That noble document that was approved on July 4, 1776, included this glorious phrase: "We hold these truths to be self-evident, that all men are created equal."

There were two things wrong with that phrase right from the start: the first was that the words "all men" were meant literally since women were not considered when the right to full citizenship, which included the right to vote, was established. That piece of unfinished business was not resolved until the passage of the Nineteenth Amendment to the U.S. Constitution in 1920. Of course, the other piece of unfinished business, some of which remains unfinished to this day, involves the status of black people in American society. When the phrase "all men are created equal" was adopted, it was understood by everyone in that room in Philadelphia in 1776 and by everyone across the newly created United States of America that the promise of equality did not extend to people of African descent.

By 1787 when the U.S. Constitution was finally ratified, there were actually two groups who were officially written out of U.S. citizenship. In article 1, section 2, paragraph 3, these interesting words are found: "Representatives and direct taxes shall be apportioned among the several States…by adding to the whole Number of free Persons, including those bound to Service for a Term of Years [white indentured servants], and excluding Indians not taxed, three fifths of all other Persons."

All white people, free and indentured, were counted as full citizens. Native Americans were not counted or considered at all. All other persons (African slaves) counted as three-fifths of a person. To determine how much in taxes a white person would pay, if that person owned slaves, they would count each five slaves as being valued as three actual persons.

The reason for the three-fifths policy was also purely political. The northern states had by then abandoned slavery and actually had fewer people than the southern states if the slave population in the South was counted. In order to keep the South from having more representatives in Congress than the northern states, they reached this political compromise: each five slaves would count as only three people. That strategy lessened taxes and political power for the southern states. Think about this: in 1776 the founders wrote and celebrated the idea that "all men" are created equal. But in 1787 they specified that black people shall count as three-fifths of a person and Indians will not be counted at all!

What were the historic effects of the three-fifths decision? In 1968, in response to the urban riots that caused many of America's cities to break out in flames between 1965–1968, President Lyndon Johnson established a study group called the Kerner Commission to determine why these urban, civil uprisings had taken place. That distinguished group of Americans reached the following conclusion: "America has become two nations, one white, one black, separate and unequal."[1] Despite the elegant language of the Declaration of Independence, the United States has followed a course of action that has resulted in inequality and disparity based on race being built into the very fabric of the nation.

That disparity has taken on a very obvious political dimension. There are fifty states in the United States of America, and today only Massachusetts has an elected black governor.[2] In the last one hundred years, only one other state (Virginia) has ever elected a black governor. There are one hundred members of the United States Senate. Today only one of them is black, and in the last 130 years, only three states have ever elected or appointed blacks to the U.S. Senate: Massachusetts, Illinois, and Mississippi, which saw two appointed by the state legislature during Reconstruction.

Nevertheless, something happened in this country on November 4, 2008, that could alter forever the course this country has been on for more than 230 years. The United States of America took a

the audacity of faith

step that I never thought I would see in my lifetime. In fact, America did something that shocked and surprised the other nations of the earth and altered our status in their eyes. On November 4, 2008, someone rose up from the three-fifths clause of the U.S. Constitution to become the person whose oath of office includes the line, "protect, preserve, and defend the Constitution of the United States."

This nation is poised to experience reconciliation after hundreds of years of racism and resistance. This nation is poised to tear down walls of division and hostility that have stood solid from one generation to another. We have gone from slavery to Jim Crow, to sharecropping, to the back of the bus, to the end of the line, to the painfully poetic line of Langston Hughes, who inquired, "What happens to a dreamed deferred?" I do not believe this is merely a "political moment." Instead, I believe this event is the biblical equivalent of God splitting the Red Sea so God's people could walk from slavery to freedom, and the equivalent of Jesus opening blind eyes and raising folks from spiritual death all at the same time. Through the election of the nation's first African American president, God is giving the United States of America one more opportunity to be reconciled after its tragic history of racial division.

Working for reconciliation is at the heart of the Christian gospel. God's central agenda in the Bible is to reconcile people with God and then reconcile people with one another. That is what Paul is talking about in 2 Corinthians 5:16-21—that God was in Christ reconciling the world to himself and has given to us the ministry of reconciliation. Nothing is more important to God than reconciliation—not preaching or tithing or worship or church growth. All of those things have occurred in a world that has remained badly, even painfully, divided. We as a nation have taken a step that George Washington and Thomas Jefferson, both slaveholders, never could have imagined: elected a black man as president of the United States of America. Somebody ought to say, "Amen"!

I confess that while the election and inauguration of Barack Obama have taken place, I am only cautiously optimistic that our country will seize upon this opportunity to move toward the reconciliation that I firmly believe is within our grasp. I don't doubt that this moment in history is poised to experience reconciliation, but America has come close to moments of racial reconciliation before, and in each instance the nation found a way or a reason to turn away from that opportunity. In 1870 the Fifteenth Amendment to the U.S. Constitution was adopted. That amendment gave the right to vote to black males, a group who slightly more than five years earlier had been living in lifelong slavery, with no notion of their even being treated as human beings. Then they were elevated to the highest level of humanity that any democracy can bestow: citizens empowered with the right to vote.

In 1870 slavery was now over, and America could have gotten on with the business of living up to the ideals of Jefferson from way back in 1776: "All men are created equal." We could have avoided so much suffering, so many lynchings, so many beatings, and so much brutality if we had only embraced that first opportunity for national racial reconciliation. But in 1870 America was not yet ready to end its affinity for being two nations, one white and one black, separate and unequal, so the problem continued. White people invented the poll tax, the grandfather clause, and the literary test, along with the blatant brutality of the KKK to keep black people away from the exercise of their rights as free citizens.

In every American military conflict since the Revolutionary War, hundreds of thousands of black men and women served in uniform while hundreds of thousands more served in support of the war effort. Surely they had proven their patriotism by their willingness to fight and die for this country. Wouldn't military service have quickly resulted in the chance to enjoy the liberty and democracy for which those men and women risked their lives? No, as many members of my congregation in Cleveland, Ohio, can attest, they returned from the front lines of a foreign war only to end up sitting in the back of the bus or standing in the back of the unemployment line or even hanging at the end of a rope when their call for freedom seemed too brash for many in white America.

We had another chance to turn a corner in this country, in 1965 when Lyndon Johnson signed the Voting Rights Act after the historic and bloody march from Selma to Montgomery, Alabama. The Civil Rights Bill had been passed in 1964, and now the right to vote was being guaranteed to all people regardless of race. The nation could have said that our long fascination with racial inequality was now over and it was time to get on with the business of being "one nation under God." But when President Johnson signed the Voting Rights Act in 1965, Senator Richard Russell of Georgia, a staunch segregationist, told Johnson that his actions would result in the southern states leaving the Democratic Party for the next one hundred years. By 1968 every southern state, and all of them had voted democratic since the Civil War, joined Richard Nixon and the Republican Party. For the next forty years, conservative politics and conservative pundits held sway in this country.

Now we are confronted with this unexpected opportunity to do something that we should have done but refused to do many times in the past. Now we have a chance to be reconciled. The signs of this potential reconciliation were embedded within Obama's campaign structure and strategy. It was thrilling to see young, white people volunteering to work for this African American candidate for president. It was amazing, almost unbelievable, to drive through white neighborhoods in my historically "red state" of Ohio and see Obama/Biden signs in the front yards.

One week before the election, as I was shopping at a Brooks Brothers store, a white customer approached me to ask if I thought "our candidate was going to win on Tuesday." He felt he had to whisper the name Obama, since that store tends to cater to a clientele that might not support the aspirations of a man seeking to become the nation's first African American president. However, assuming that I was also a supporter of Obama (not all black people were), he made it clear to me that Obama was his choice as well. Just days before the election, several former Republican officials for both Bush and Reagan, most notably General Colin Powell, announced their support for this candidate from the former three-fifths community. This moment in history was nothing short of miraculous.

Nevertheless, the power of hatred and prejudice is strong, and some people were not able to bring themselves to cast a vote for Obama. In my opinion, the color of Obama's skin was the only reason why that election was close. Given a bad economy, a costly and unpopular war, and a Republican president with the lowest approval ratings of any president in the last one hundred years, one was left to wonder why it was that Obama did not lead his Republican opponent by fifteen to twenty points as they went into Election Day. The answer may be contained in the title of the book Cornel West wrote back in 1994, *Race Matters*!

This nation did, however, take a step that can help us reverse our painful and tragic past and set us on a path toward being a reconciled community. We can embrace this opportunity that God has once again given us, and we can finally affirm that "all men and all women are created equal." The election of Barack Obama is not only about the possibilities of our future; it is also about outgrowing and moving beyond the self-imposed limitations of our past. America electing a black man to be its president was bigger than politics; it was a transformational moment in national history. This country and this world will never be the same if we are willing and able to embrace the possibility of racial reconciliation that God has set before us.

Such reconciliation *is* possible, especially when it involves people who are in Christ. Paul says, "If anyone is in Christ, there is a new creation: everything old has passed away; see, everything has become new!" (2 Corinthians 5:17). When people come to Christ, old things ought to pass away. Old prejudices, old biases, and old bigotries ought to pass away. The color of a person's skin ought not to matter. All that should matter is the red blood of Christ that was shed to cleanse us from sin and free us to embrace a future where there is no longer Jew or Gentile, no longer slave or free, no longer male and female (Galatians 3:28).

No gap was wider in all of history than the emotional gap between men and women, Jews and Gentiles, and slaves and free people in the ancient Greco-Roman world. Those divisions were as deep as anything we have faced in this country. Yet, as people

the audacity of faith

began to relate and respond to one another under the guidance of the Holy Spirit and under the influence of the teachings of Jesus Christ, they were able to operate outside of their old paradigms of prejudice. Jesus was even able to bring about such reconciliation within the ranks of his own disciples. He brought a tax collector like Matthew who worked for the Romans and a political zealot like Simon who worked to overthrow the Romans into his original group of twelve disciples. In Christ, reconciliation becomes the order of the day.

If reconciliation can work in South Africa after the collapse of the apartheid regime, it can work anywhere. They established something in that country called the Truth and Reconciliation Commission. They understood that former enemies could not share the country together after Nelson Mandela became the president unless and until they could be reconciled. However, after centuries of white minority rule through the most brutal of policies and practices, reconciliation seemed easier said than done. Then Bishop Desmond Tutu came up with this idea: if those who inflicted the suffering would simply tell the truth about what they had done, then those who had experienced the suffering would be willing to forgive and reconciliation could occur.

Imagine the scene as former South African police took the stand and confessed to the survivors of the victims they had kidnapped, tortured, brutalized, and hanged. Then imagine those survivors going to the very men who had killed their loved ones and shaking their hands as a sign of forgiveness and reconciliation. That is how South Africa was able to survive after a long history of racial division; Bishop Tutu led them through the ministry of reconciliation.

If South Africans can be reconciled, we in the United States can be reconciled as well. We do not have long to wait to see if our nation is ready. If we let this chance slip away, we may not get another chance like this for a long time. Look beyond the political issues of health care and foreign policy and which party is going to control the government. This election is a test of something much more substantive and much more elusive; it is a test of the very character of our country. This is our chance to see if America is finally ready to live up to the words that have eluded us since 1776: "We hold these truths to be self-evident, that all men are created equal."

Less than one month after President Obama had been inaugurated, the *New York Post* ran what many condemned as a crude and tasteless political cartoon. It pictured two white police officers who had just shot a monkey, and the cartoon text commented on the next round of economic stimulus plans for the country.[3] That cartoon served as a clear reminder that for some in America the election of the first black president is not a welcomed event. One conservative radio talk show program featured a caller who said that as far as he was concerned, "the White House was not nearly white enough for him." Despite all of the hatred and prejudice and bigotry, an election was held, and America is poised to write a new and exciting chapter in its history. Whether we follow through on this opportunity remains to be seen.

Barack Obama ran for and won the office of president of the United States because he was possessed by the *audacity of hope*. He believed that he could achieve that goal, no matter how impossible it may have seemed to most Americans on the day he announced his candidacy. Now that Obama has been elected by the *audacity of his hope*, it falls to all of us in this country to lay claim to the reconciliation that is within our grasp as a direct result of this historic election through the *audacity of our faith*. As the old spiritual invites us to sing: "Sinner, please don't let this harvest pass."

NOTES

1. Read the full text of this report at http://www.eisenhowerfoundation.org/docs/kerner.pdf (accessed March 17, 2009).

2. On March 17, 2008, upon the resignation of New York Governor Eliot Spitzer, Lieutenant Governor David Paterson was sworn in as the state's first African American governor, bringing this nation's current number of black governors to two.

3. Earlier in the same week when the cartoon appeared, a pet chimpanzee had had to be shot by police after it attacked the neighbor of its Connecticut owner. In an apology printed the day after the cartoon's publication, the *New York Post* acknowledged the controversy, denied any racist intent, and asserted the cartoon mocked only an "ineptly written" economic stimulus bill.

PART I
My Soul Looks Back and Wonders How We Got Over

1
AT LAST!

LESLIE D. CALLAHAN

Inauguration Day, January 20, 2009, was filled with unforgettable images—from the tearful Representative John Lewis, to the regal Aretha Franklin and her stylish hat, to the elegant and intelligent new First Lady, Michelle Obama, and the confident and smiling new president of the United States of America, Barack Hussein Obama. Whether journeyed to Washington to huddle in the cold with 2 million others or remained at home to watch the proceedings on TV or the Internet, together we witnessed things that were both unseen and unheard of before that day.

For me the most striking image associated with Obama's inauguration came from the creative mind of the artist John Mavroudis, whose imagined inauguration provides the cover illustration for the February 2, 2009, edition of *The Nation* magazine. His piece envisions the inauguration witnessed not "in flesh and blood, but in the bonds of justice and peace."[1] In that illustration President Obama is depicted receiving the oath of office from Thurgood Marshall, famed attorney for the NAACP and the first African American to serve as an associate justice of the United States Supreme Court. Also present in the gallery are Martin Luther King Jr., whose prophetic witness called upon America to make good on its promises. Emmett Till, the black teenager from Chicago who was brutally murdered in Mississippi in 1955, is on hand, along with Denise McNair, Addie Mae Collins, Carole Robertson, and Cynthia Wesley, the "four little girls" murdered by the terrorist bombing of Birmingham's 16th Street Baptist Church in 1963. W. E. B. DuBois, who prophesied about the twentieth-century problem of the color line, is present, as is Dred Scott, who was told in the nineteenth century that his blackness was an insurmountable barrier to U.S. citizenship. Shirley Chisholm, who ran for president in 1972, is in the group, along with Harriet Tubman, whom her people called "Moses." These and so many other freedom fighters and history makers of every hue and creed, were shown by Mavroudis as a great cloud of witnesses and a historic chorus gathered together to celebrate the inauguration of the nation's first black president.

During the actual inauguration, Rev. Dr. Joseph Lowery evoked this sense of continuity by beginning his benediction with the third verse of James Weldon Johnson's famous hymn, known by many as the Negro National Anthem, "Lift Every Voice and Sing":

> God of our weary years,
> God of our silent tears,
> Thou who has brought us thus far on the way;
> Thou who has by Thy might
> Led us into the light,
> Keep us forever in the path, we pray.
> Lest our feet stray from the places, our God,
>   where we met Thee,
> Lest our hearts drunk with the wine of the world,
>   we forget Thee;
> Shadowed beneath Thy hand,
> May we forever stand,
> True to our God,
> True to our native land.

Elizabeth Alexander, the poet selected for the occasion, also claimed the memories of those whose labors and deaths made the moment possible: "Sing the names of the dead who brought us here."[2] Praiseworthy it is to have come this far, not only as black people but also as Americans. And fitting it is to remember that this journey did not begin with the announcement of Barack Obama's candidacy, nor did it end with his election and inauguration. Much that happened on Inauguration Day, but especially Lowery's prayer, Alexander's poem, and Mavroudis's image, emphasized the historical movements, the human labor, and the creativity and sacrifice that made that celebration possible. On the day of the inauguration, we heard a national sigh of relief that was embodied and performed at the Neighborhood Ball when President and Mrs. Obama danced their first dance to "At Last," performed by Beyoncé who was inspired by Etta James. At last we have broken through the racial barrier and elected a black president to be at the head of our government. Well into the twentieth century our military was segregated, but at the end of the first decade of the twenty-first century, the commander in chief is black. At last there is a black family in the White House, and they are not just the staff. At last we are realizing some of our promise as a republic.

All of the sights and sounds of that day, from YoYo Ma and his musical ensemble to the first strains of "Hail to the Chief," represented this mighty exhalation at the end of a long journey—ah, at last.

> Stony the road we trod,
> Bitter the chast'ning rod,
> Felt in the days when hope unborn had died;
> Yet with a steady beat,
> Have not our weary feet
> Come to the place for which our fathers sighed?
> We have come over a way that with tears has
>   been watered,
> We have come, treading our path through the blood
>   of the slaughtered,
> Out from the gloomy past,
> 'Til now we stand *at last*
> Where the white gleam of our bright star is cast.

On that day of celebration and promise, the yearnings of the historical chorus found a part of their answer, at last.

At the same time, as we engage this crucial moment through the lens of fulfillment, we recognize much for which we still wait and work. We still wait for the emergence of economic stability, not just for the few but for all. We still wait for the promise of universal health care. We still wait for all people to have productive and meaningful labor at a living wage. We still wait for real peace in the Middle East, which includes justice for the Palestinians and security for the Israelis. We still wait for solutions to the crises that afflict war-torn areas around the world, especially the Sudan. We wait for prosperity for Haiti. And we still wait for a woman to break some executive glass ceilings, especially of the presidency. After all, we elected Barack Obama president with the hope that he will advance progressive policies toward a just and prosperous nation; we did not welcome the Messiah to usher in the millennial reign. Here now we stand, at last, in celebration, but still waiting and with much good work still to do.

In truth, no one knows the tremendous task at hand better nor has articulated it more eloquently than President Obama himself in his inaugural address. In the midst of the celebration and with striking solemnity, he uttered these words: "What is required of us now is a new era of responsibility—a recognition, on the part of every American, that we have duties to ourselves, our nation and the world; duties that we do not grudgingly accept but rather seize gladly, firm in the knowledge that there is nothing so satisfying to the spirit, so defining of our character, than giving our all to a difficult task."[3]

The tension of the already but not yet is the story of black history, and it is also central to the biblical tradition. James Weldon Johnson expressed this tension as he penned the words that have inspired and encouraged generations of black Americans. Writing more than a century ago, at the height of segregation and lynching, but also in an era of black progress he said that his generation had "come to the place for which our fathers [and mothers] sighed." Johnson's words certainly embodied the recognition that we have

the audacity of faith

come a long way but still have a long way to go. Considering this reminds us all that the inauguration of Barack Obama is not the first pivotal historical moment for black people or for our country. When the Emancipation Proclamation went into effect, slaves and their allies sighed, "At last." At university commencements marking the completion of dreamed of educational journeys, newly minted black doctors, lawyers, teachers, and their families sighed, "At last." Following the landmark Supreme Court rulings that overturned the "separate but equal" doctrine and desegregated public schools, public accommodations, and public transportation, freedom fighters and their lawyers sighed, "At last." With the passage of the Civil Rights Bill and the Voting Rights Act, African Americans and other people of goodwill celebrated with the words "At last." Despite the reasonable exultation at their victories, however, in every case our ancestors recognized then what we must acknowledge now: that the struggle not only continues, but that it frequently becomes more arduous in the wake of such significant strides.

Psalm 126, a psalm believed to derive from the Jewish experience of returning from the Babylonian exile in the sixth century BCE, beautifully represents the tension of celebrating the fulfillment of dreams amidst the continuing challenges of the present and future. The first verses resonate with the jubilance that gripped African Americans when President Obama was elected and inaugurated. Like the Jews at their time of restoration, "We were like those who dream. Then our mouth was filled with laughter, and our tongue with shouts of joy" (vv. 1-2). In churches all over the nation, the chorus sounded, "The LORD has done great things for us, and we rejoiced" (v. 3). More than just the culmination of a single individual's strivings and ambitions, Barack Obama's election felt like a divine gift to black America, and our celebration felt holy.

In the second part of Psalm 126, though, we are left with the work that follows the answer to prayers. Indeed, we are left to pray new prayers to accompany our new assignment. The restoration celebrated in verse 1 remains incomplete in verse 4, as the psalmist asks, "Restore our fortunes, O Lord." But even then the psalmist makes clear that the work is not God's alone. So while asking the

Lord to complete the restoration, the psalmist also includes a blessing for the human laborers, "May those who sow with tears reap with shouts of joy" (v. 5). Finally, the psalm closes with the hope that although the rebuilding would be demanding and even painful, its labor would bear fruit, shouts of joy, and sheaves of wheat (v. 6).

Without question, African Americans along with other justice-minded people have reckoned the election and the inauguration of Barack Hussein Obama as the culmination of a long journey from exile to full citizenship and as an answer to prayers. It has occasioned tears and shouts of joy for what has already occurred, an event that many of us never imagined to see in our lifetime. But wise people know and Christians proclaim that the last verse of the freedom song, though in process, has not yet been completed. Thus, like our ancestors, we continue to sing of freedom and celebrate its promises, while we yet labor in hope for its advent at last.

> Lift every voice and sing,
> 'Til earth and heaven ring,
> Ring with the harmonies of Liberty;
> Let our rejoicing rise
> High as the listening skies,
> Let it resound loud as the rolling sea.
> Sing a song full of the faith that the dark past has
>   taught us,
> Sing a song full of the hope that the present has
>   brought us;
> Facing the rising sun of our new day begun,
> Let us march on 'til victory is won.

NOTES

1. "Inauguration for the Ages," *The Nation*, January 14, 2009, http://www.thenation.com/doc/20090202/key.

2. Elizabeth Alexander, "Praise Song for the Day," http://www.nytimes.com/2009/01/20/us/politics/20text-poem.html?ref=books.

3. Quoted from Barack Obama's inaugural address, http://www.nytimes.com/2009/01/20/us/politics/20text-obama.html (accessed March 17, 2009).

2
GOD'S INVISIBLE HAND

J. ALFRED SMITH SR.

The religious right speaks about returning America to the Christian principles on which America was founded. The founders of the country were products of the Enlightenment that elevated human logic and reason. They were deists who believed that the universe had a creator, but that this creative power did not concern itself with humans, either by revelation or sacred books. These deists spoke of nature's God, or the God of nature. Deists believed that after creating the world and giving it the natural laws it needed to function, this God left the world to function on its own.

This God, who should not be understood as the personal God of Christianity, is like an absentee landlord or a watchmaker who no longer has any interest in his creation. Deism was strong in the seventeenth and eighteenth centuries and was popular in the thinking of Thomas Jefferson, Benjamin Franklin, James Madison, John Adams, and Alexander Hamilton. However, some argue that George Washington spoke about "the smiles of providence."[1]

The religious right, according to the polls, did not favor the election of Barack Obama prior to the election, because they saw him as a far left extremist. The Christian Anti-Defamation Commission posted videos called "7 Reasons Why Barack Obama Is Not a Christian." Focus on the Family issued a family action letter signed by "A Christian from 2012." This letter predicted awful events that would take place if Barack Obama was elected. Talk radio host Rush Limbaugh made Mr. Obama appear as the Antichrist, as did the religious right, moderate evangelicals, white bread Protestants, conservative Catholics, and the Latter-day Saints

(Mormons). Their preference for the presidency was Senator John McCain. Meanwhile, black Protestants, Jews, Muslims, and the American secular community saw Barack Obama as one who could unify a divided nation and give hope to a nation intoxicated with hopelessness.

The chances of winning first the Democratic nomination and then the general election did not look too good for Barack Obama. He had a great many obstacles arrayed against him.

1. Religious people did not trust him.

2. His name was a problem for patriotic Americans: Barack Hussein Obama.

3. His Muslim relatives in Indonesia troubled antiterrorist American warriors.

4. His youthful age suggested to some a lack of maturity.

5. His lack of executive experience made him seem unqualified.

6. His prophetic pastor of twenty years was a problem, as was his connection to the 1960s radical Bill Ayres.

7. The most liberal member of the U.S. Senate, he started a campaign with little money (but rich with faith, hope, and love).

8. No black person had ever been elected U.S. president.

Yes, the opposition built a hot bonfire to burn Barack Obama with blistering criticism. But the hotter they made the fire, the cooler and calmer he was in his responses. Some African American Christians saw the mean-spirited attacks, and all we could do was pray for him. All we could do was to thank God for Mrs. Obama for helping him and for their two daughters for consoling him. All we could do was pray for his safety.

As voices of hatred arose to demonize Barack Obama, some of Allen Temple's members began to fear for Brother Obama's safety. They remembered what happened to Dr. Martin Luther King Jr. and to Medgar Evers. They could not forget the untimely and unnecessary deaths of brothers Robert Kennedy and John F. Kennedy. They said to me, "Pastor, we don't want him to run for office. America is not ready for a black person to be the president."

Well, God had to make God's move. God had to trouble the waters that had been stale and stagnant. God had to stir up the tidal waves of change. Young white people, young black people, and people tired of partisan politics felt a tide in the affairs of American history. They could sense intuitively the presence and power of God at work in Barack Obama. God, who pulls down rulers from their thrones and elevates humble persons to places of power, had anointed a humble, poor man with an African father and a white American mother to lead and heal on the world stage. As Julius Caesar once observed, "There is a tide in the affairs of men (and women), which, taken at the flood leads on to fortune; omitted, all the voyage of their life is bound in shallows and miseries. On such a full sea are we now afloat. And we must take the current when it serves or lose our ventures."[2]

Barack Obama has taken the current because the tide is in and the sea is full. He cannot complete the journey all by himself. Let us join President Obama and be God's hands and hearts for helping and healing. Don't be afraid of leaving the security of the shore. Find your place with the crew. Don't say I am too small. Do your part no matter how small. "Little is much if God is in it." God, who drags down strong rulers and puts humble people in places of power, has a place for you. The sea may be big, but the ship is strong and the Captain is brave.

We do not fear the surge of the sea or the leap of the waves of opposition. Let not the flickering flash of lightning disturb the sky of our emotions. Let not the loud thunderclap of human debate deafen our ears so that we cannot hear God's voice within our souls. Let not the demons of the devil pour like torrential rains upon our worldview so that our vision is blurred and our view is distorted. Let not sinful storms bring hurricanes of discouragement, and let not the music of an evil wind sing disturbing melodies of falsehoods. God is with us in our history. The sea may be big, but the ship is strong and Jesus our Captain is brave.

I would not be a Christian if God's invisible hand could not redeem me. A religion without redemption is a religion without salvation. A religion without salvation is a religion without good news. Without good news is a religion without hope, and hope is the promise of God for a better future. When hope dies, the pregnant mother of time dies with the unborn child of a redeemed future. But the invisible hand of God redeems our future by redeeming our present. God enters the delivery room of time and calls on us to assist the mother of "The Fading Now" in the delivery of the baby called "Almost but Not Yet." God's invisible hand is reaching out to touch people who will assist God in giving birth to love, justice, and peace.

> This is my Father's world, O let me ne'er forget
> That though the wrong seems oft so strong
> God is the Ruler yet.
> This is my Father's world, the battle is not done.
> Jesus who died shall be satisfied,
> And earth and heaven be one.[3]

Yes, this is the world where God's invisible hand is working. God's hand moves in world history. That is why Mahalia Jackson sang, "He's got the whole world in his hands." God's hand moves in your life and in mine. God's hand leads; God's hand guides; God's hand protects. God's hand raised up Jesus from an obscure birth in Bethlehem, from refugee status in Africa, and from a carpenter's shop in Nazareth. God raised up Jesus from the Jordan to a salvation mission in a lost world. When good folk and bad folk, when the Jerusalem righteous and the Roman military lifted him high to mock him unto death, and then low enough to bury him in a borrowed tomb, God brought down Herod, Pilate, Caesar, the high priests, and the military cruelty of Rome. Then God elevated Jesus high enough so that the name of Jesus is higher than every name, and at the name of Jesus every knee must bow and every tongue must confess that he is Lord!

NOTES
   1. http://tpmcafe.talkingpointsmemo.com/2008/03/10/fallacy_1_the_founders _werent/ (accessed March 17, 2009).
   2. Julius Caesar, act 4, scene 3.
   3. Maltbie D. Babcock, "This Is My Father's World," public domain.

the audacity of faith

3

THE HOPEOLOGY OF BARACK OBAMA:
Biblical Reflections and Personal Musings

MITZI J. SMITH

For the first time in my life, I was *really* proud of my home state of Ohio. I shouted, cried, and danced on November 4 when MSNBC called Ohio for Barack Obama. A majority vote from the residents of the "red state" of Ohio signaled an anticipated Obama victory. I grew up in Columbus. I judged blacks in Columbus as generally pessimistic, culturally detached, and politically alienated. I resolved that only a miracle could persuade a majority of Ohio's 22 percent black population to vote for Obama. And I certainly would not have bet on Obama winning the majority of the white vote. I remember, as one of few black children in my elementary school, how, during recess, my white schoolmates played with my braids and chatted about how soft they felt. As a teenager working in a retail credit agency, I recall that my age did not deter a white adult female coworker from capriciously calling me a "nigger." The law clerk of the legal firm that employed me as a legal secretary confessed that prior to hiring me they never would have employed a black woman because "we just assumed they were too slow." I know painfully well about the "hope gaps"[1] in Columbus. Obama inspired millions of Americans to a renewed hope in our common humanity and in our ability to bridge the gaps of hope.

Like the common cold, pessimism, negativity, and fear can be infectious and debilitating. And like laughter, optimism, and confidence, hope can be contagious and invigorating. The right words aptly spoken can inspire people to exchange nightmares for dreams. As Obama has affirmed, "There is power in words ...there is power in conviction...there is power in hope."[2] Some situations are so ominous and paralyzing that we yearn for an external word of hope. A "dumb"[3] and costly war; significant and steady job losses; record foreclosures and homelessness; dwindling retirement funds; deceitful, divisive, and incompetent government; unprecedented gasoline prices; and more contribute to despair and alienation among Americans.

King Zedekiah inquired of Jeremiah, "Is there any word from the LORD?" (Jeremiah 37:17). The psalmist declared, "I rise before dawn and cry for help; I put my hope in your words" (Psalm 119:147). Obama witnessed "the Word" manifested "in the day-to-day work of men and women [he] met in church each day, in their ability to 'make a way out of no way' and maintain hope and dignity in the direst of circumstances."[4]

The creed "The Lord will make a way out of no way" is both an individual and communal expression of faith in God's proven ability to do the impossible. God does not do for us what we can do for ourselves. The hope that Obama challenged Americans to seize rests on the conviction that individual and collective effort produce change. When Obama announced his candidacy, he asserted, "We all make this journey for a reason....In the face of despair, you believe there can be hope. In the face of a politics that's shut you out, that's told you to settle, that's divided us for too long, you believe *we* can be one people."[5] His repetitive communal summons invited Americans to collective engagement: "*Let's* build a government" that works for all people; "*Let's* rebuild our country"; "*We* can build a more hopeful America" (italics added).

Americans share a common history, citizenship, humanity, dreams, and faith that function as wellsprings of our hope. The theme of collective engagement is woven throughout the biblical text. When the exilic prophet Nehemiah returned to his homeland of Judah to rebuild the walls of Jerusalem, he persuaded the people of their vested interest in the rebuilding project. Nehemiah rallied the people to collective engagement: "'You see the trouble *we* are in....Come, let *us* rebuild the wall of Jerusalem, so that *we* may

the audacity of faith

no longer suffer disgrace.' Then they said, 'Let *us* start building!' So they committed themselves to *the common good*" (Nehemiah 2:17-18, emphasis added).

In the apostle Paul's first letter to the "saints" in Corinth, he addressed a rumor from "Chloe's people" about divisions among them (1 Corinthians 1:11-12). Paul highlighted the diversity and indispensability of their individual and collective gifts. He invoked the image of the human body as a paradigm for the inner workings of the church as the "body of Christ": "For just as the body is one and has many members, and all the members of the body, though many, are one body, so it is with Christ" (1 Corinthians 12:12). President Obama seems to have tapped into this Pauline concept when he said, "America is more than the sum of its parts—out of many, we are truly one."[6] We have a stake in one another's success or failure. Despite our differences, "we rise and fall together."[7] As Paul reasoned, "If one member suffers, all suffer together with it; if one member is honored, all rejoice together with it" (v. 26).

Differently from Obama, Paul elevated love above faith and hope (1 Corinthians 13:13). He admonished the Corinthians against the hierarchical ordering of their gifts; they should exercise them in love. Otherwise, they resemble "a noisy gong or a clanging cymbal" (1 Corinthians 13:1). Obama does not invoke the word "love"; he employs common religious parlance that signifies love: "What is called for is nothing more, and nothing less, than what all the world's great religions demand—that we do unto others as we would have them do unto us." Obama proclaimed, "Let us be our brother's keeper; Let us be our sister's keeper. Let us find that common stake we all have in one another, and let our politics reflect that spirit as well."[8] Paul declared, "And now faith, hope, and love abide; these three" (1 Corinthians 13:13). But Obama advises that "the greatest gift we can pass on to our children [is] the gift of hope....We do what we can to build our house upon the sturdiest rock. And when the winds come, and the rains fall, and they beat upon that house, we keep faith that our Father will be there to guide us, and watch over us, and protect us, and lead His children through the darkest of storms into the light of a better day."[9]

We can create that better day. Obama characterizes American history and contemporary life in terms of "paradox and promise." Our founding documents cradle an embryonic promise of a "perfect union." Presently, "we see through a glass, darkly" (1 Corinthians 13:12 KJV). The Constitution "promised its people liberty, justice, and a union that could be and should be perfected over time."[10] Yet, Obama affirmed, while that constitution was insufficient to end the enslavement and disenfranchisement of slaves and people of color; successive generations of Americans would protest and struggle to "narrow that gap between the promise of our ideals and the reality of their time."[11] On February 2007 while speaking in Springfield, Illinois, Obama proposed that we "take up the unfinished business of perfecting *our* nation....Together *we* can." Our past achievements propel us to have "the audacity to hope—for what we can and must achieve tomorrow."[12] For African Americans "that path means embracing the burdens of our past without becoming victims of our past. It means continuing to insist on a full measure of justice in every aspect of American life."[13]

This unfinished business also necessitates the creation of a "new declaration of independence" in our collective and individual hearts. This new creation requires a "change of hearts and minds manifest in real change for the benefit of all."[14] The Lord told the prophet Jeremiah: "The days are surely coming...when I will make a new covenant with the house of Israel and the house of Judah. It will not be like the covenant that I made with their ancestors when I took them by the hand to bring them out of the land of Egypt— a covenant that they broke....But...I will put my law within them, and *I will write it on their hearts*; and I will be their God, and they shall be my people" (Jeremiah 31:31-33, emphasis added). This new declaration of independence etched in our hearts and minds will produce concrete "flesh and blood" change.

For me Obama's candidacy and election embody a flesh and blood paradigm of hope. "Hope—hope—is what led me here today—with a father from Kenya; a mother from Kansas; and a story that could only happen in America," Obama testified.[15]

the audacity of faith

Played on the global stage, Obama's candidacy manifested audacious hope: "Hope in the face of difficulty; hope in the face of uncertainty."[16] When Obama embarked on this journey, he lacked the financial capital of his opponents, the name recognition of the Clintons, and the backing of many influential Clinton loyalists (black, white, Latino, and others). Some blacks refused to support Obama because they feared for his life and/or because they believed he could not garner sufficient white votes. Others suggested Obama's Harvard Law School training predisposed him to elitism.[17] Some blacks decreed he was not "black enough,"[18] having ordained Clinton the "first black president"! Obama confessed, "I do not fit the typical pedigree."

"Faith is the substance of things hoped for, the evidence of things not seen" (Hebrews 11:1 KJV). We put too much stock in things seen. Defining and defending the audacity to hope in the future possibilities of America, Obama argued:

> Hope is not blind optimism. It's not ignoring the enormity of the task before us or the roadblocks that stand in our path....Hope has been the guiding force behind the most improbable changes this country has ever made. In the face of tyranny, it's what led a band of colonists to rise up against an empire. In the face of slavery, it's what fueled the resistance of the slave and the abolitionist....In the face of oppression, it's what led young men and women to sit at lunch counters and brave fire hoses and march through the streets of Selma and Montgomery for freedom's cause. That's the power of hope—to imagine and then work for what had seemed impossible before. Hope is that thing inside us that insists, despite all evidence to the contrary, that something better is waiting for us around the corner. But only if we're willing to work for it and fight for it.[19]

Hope is the soil in which we plant seeds of faith. Hope without faith is deficient and fragile optimism. Faith without hope is blind ambition. And "faith apart from works is barren" (James 2:20).

Hebrews 12:4-40 chronicles women and men from Abel to Rahab, and from Gideon to unnamed women who married faith with work to overcome life's paradoxes and to seize the hoped-for promise. "We are surrounded by so great a cloud of witnesses" (v. 1): Harriet Tubman, Sojourner Truth, Hiram Revels, Fannie Lou Hamer, John Lewis, Shirley Chisholm, President Barack H. Obama, and First Lady Michelle Obama. So let us "hold firmly to the hope that we confess."[20]

NOTES

1. Barack H. Obama, "Selma Voting Rights March Commemoration," Selma, AL, March 4, 2007, in *In His Own Words: Barack Obama's Speeches 2007 + 2008. The American Promise*, comp. Susan A. Jones (CreateSpace, 2008). Hereafter, I will identify all quotations from Obama speeches that are included in this compilation by the name, place, and date of the speech.

2. Obama, "Announcement for President," Springfield, IL, February 10, 2007.

3. Barack Obama, "Against Going to War with Iraq," Chicago, IL, October 2, 2002. http://en.wikisource.org/wiki/Barack_Obama's_Iraq_Speech (accessed March 17, 2009).

4. Obama, *The Audacity of Hope: Thoughts on Reclaiming the American Dream* (New York: Crown, 2006), 207.

5. Obama, "Announcement for President" (italics added).

6. Obama, "A More Perfect Union," Philadelphia, March 18, 2009.

7. Obama, *Audacity of Hope*, 193.

8. Obama, "A More Perfect Union."

9. Obama, "Remarks of Senator Barack Obama: Apostolic Church of God," Chicago, June 15, 2008.

10. Obama, "A More Perfect Union."

11. Ibid.

12. Ibid.

13. Ibid.

14. Barack Obama, speech on inaugural train ride from Philadelphia to Washington, DC, January 17, 2009.

15. Obama, "Remarks of Senator Barack Obama: Iowa Caucus Night," Des Moines, January 3, 2008.

16. Obama, speech at 2004 Democratic National Convention.

17. A dilemma shared by many minorities training at Ivy League schools, including this author.

18. Obama, *Audacity of Hope*, 210.

19. Obama, "Our Moment Is Now," remarks made in Des Moines, December 27, 2007.

20. Obama, "Announcement for President."

4
BARACK OBAMA AND THE UNFINISHED BUSINESS OF AMERICA

CHRIS RICE

The presidency of Barack Obama marks indisputable progress in American society and the end of certain debates about race. Whether it was a matter of finally allowing character and excellence to trump skin color, or a new generation that embraces multiethnicity, enough white people have changed to support a black man as their leader. I suspect that the hearts and minds of many Americans will be further changed by witnessing the Obama marriage and family, an up-close introduction to a black family that will defy stereotypes reinforced by a lack of interracial friendships. The debate has also ended as to whether African Americans have gained significant power in America, for the most powerful person in the world is Barack Obama.

Yet these new racial facts highlight all the more a strange paradox: making progress toward assimilating into mainstream power is not the same as experiencing racial reconciliation and the beloved community. Three challenges illuminate the difference.

First, if many whites have become less racist and many blacks have gained power, together this "new mainstream" increasingly isolates itself from America's poor. What is true in my city of Durham, North Carolina, seems true everywhere: 90 percent of gun murders occur in neglected communities of color, and people of all races and all churches are largely abandoning these communities. Furthermore, the new multiethnic mainstream does not seem disturbed by the new American segregation—we have the highest incarceration rate in the world and no social imagination about redeeming those in prison and the communities they come from. The force of exclusion is shifting from race to haves and have-nots, with profound results at the margins. An African American pastor of an interracial church in inner-city Atlanta tells me that longtime neighborhood residents and the transplants (white, Asian American, Latino, and black) who have made the neighborhood their home for the sake of shalom and solidarity are creating a "new we" more powerful than ethnic identities.

A second challenge of racial reconciliation was revealed at a May 2008 gathering of U.S. peace and justice leaders at Duke Divinity School. The hottest issue that emerged was not about black-white but about immigration and the black-brown divide. One black pastor's honest admission—"My people don't view immigration raids as our issue"—opened a candid and fresh conversation that led to redefinitions about who "our people" are. Since then this pastor has helped ignite a new interracial grassroots coalition addressing immigration issues in Houston.

These first two challenges both point to the unfinished business of the civil rights movement: moving from integration to koinonia and joyful repentance across racial and socio-economic divider. Sharing spaces of everyday interracial life and pursuing God's shalom together in local places is the deeper, more beautiful and transformational vision whose absence continues to impoverish us all. Nowhere is this absence seen more vividly than in America's segregated Sabbath which has accepted the racial and economic homogenization of the church as inevitable. Somehow we came to believe that we can experience God's new creation without experiencing one another's company as brothers and sisters. We still don't desire one another's company in the intimate mutuality of worshiping together weekly, reading the Bible and praying together, eating together, and ministering at the margins together as allies for the sake of the gospel.

In this respect, the hope I am holding on to for Obama's leadership is the depth and candor of his Philadelphia speech on race and the fact that his most fundamental racial identity seems to be his being biracial. He represents a new generation of children of interracial families who have experienced the rich gifts and real challenges of finding intimacy across the divide, who refuse to choose between the cultures of their two parents. They want the best of both, see the flaws of self-sufficiency, and are willing to lose some friends along the way for the sake of their desire for something better than the old categories of who "my people" are.

At the same time, the Messiah has not yet returned, and we must not forget a fundamental difference between Obama and Dr. King. One is a politician whose bottom-line interest is what's best for America. The other was a prophet whose driving concern was discerning and preaching the will of God, whatever it cost him. Let us not hope for too much.

In the final analysis, having a person like Barack Obama as president, neither black nor white, may point us to what it looks like to embrace the harder, deeper work of mutuality and koinonia, which is the church's unfinished business. Our communities and congregations need to look more like him.

5
DREAMING LIKE A FOOL

ROBIN L. SMITH

Years ago when I was considering a new business endeavor, a man I was dating disrespectfully made fun of me, saying, "Robin, you are dreaming like a fool." He would have been right if the dream had come from my ego, but this was God's plan and mission for my life. I had been called to a work bigger than I understood or could have imagined. My job was to show up, and God's job was to reveal his plan on a "need to know" basis. It is not uncommon for those called into God's service to appear as dreaming fools to others. Hebrews 11 is filled with testimonies of God making possible what seemed impossible.

God gives dreams and visions to men and women that the world might be healed, not to massage the ego of any individual, family, or political dynasty. The challenge is that there is a price for being the ethical fool who knows the truth and who speaks that truth to people in power. This has often led to political suicide, assassinations, and in the case of Jesus, to crucifixion.

The 2008 presidential election of Barack Hussein Obama, the forty-fourth president of the United States of America, began in the minds of many like someone dreaming like a fool, hallucinating, having delusions of grandeur or possibly a full-blown psychotic episode. Did this young, highly educated man actually think as a freshman senator that he could become the president of the United States of America? Yes, he did! He was not crazy and he was not dreaming like a fool. This was God's hand moving within the framework of time to bring about a necessary change within humanity.

President Obama was called a mutt and a half-breed with Kansas and Kenyan blood blended from the batter of a white, working-class woman and a black East African man. There are those who are hungry for him and his administration to fail. In fact, losing his dignity and smile are at the top of many agendas. Are we insane? Is our nation so diseased that we are still willing to pursue our historic attraction to profit even at the expense of watching while people lose their homes, their jobs, and their hopes? It is not the American dream that is sick; the sickness resides with its citizens. We ought to make a citizen's arrest for anyone choosing the demise of our nation over the opportunity for all to thrive. The culture is spiritually sick, limping from the error of its ways. We need the wisest and most seasoned souls to help heal our nation just as much as we need the best financial minds to repair our broken economy. Given the devastation that has raped the land, any American or human who would wish failure on this new president is a sadist.

Dr. King's dream of "we as a people will get to the Promised Land" certainly encompassed the election of an African American president, but his dream reached much deeper into healing the psyche of racism, sexism, ageism, and disregard for the poor both in this country and around the world. President Obama's victory was a significant move on the chessboard of life, but it was only the first step toward overcoming the debilitating disease that has infected America at its core and paralyzed its pursuit of becoming a "more perfect union."

The attackers of both Dr. King and President Obama forgot to do a background check on them. Not about their parents and extended families, but their foreparents on whose shoulders they stood. Being beaten and jailed unjustly, spat on, kicked, battered with water hoses, and living with death threats was familiar territory to those freedom fighters. The terroristic murder of four innocent girls in Sunday school when the 16th Street Baptist Church in Birmingham was bombed was a reminder for us all that racial hatred creates monsters out of insecure and spiritually crippled human beings.

Dreaming like a fool is what all men and women look like who have gotten a call on the "bat" phone from God in the middle of the day or midnight hour asking one question: "Will you go for me? There is something that needs my attention, and the time is now." Note that it is God calling the meeting, setting the agenda, and executing the plan. The role of President Obama, Dr. King, you, or me is to be available to perform the tasks that have been assigned us, nothing more or less.

"Go where?" the dreamer asks. God might tell us: "Go into the valley where only the echo of the cries from the poor, disinherited, hungry, illiterate, drug addicted, and bruised in spirit, are living. Go to them, for they only hear themselves. The world has turned a deaf and unresponsive ear to them, in its silence blaming them for problems that those of privilege have created. Go tell them that Health and Human Services are coming to them, and tell them that while budgets are getting cut and corporate bailouts are on the rise, I have not forgotten them and their need for a habitat fit for humanity. All they hear is the resounding chatter of their own powerless voices. No one is listening to them, no one even knows that they are still in the crevices and cracks in the valley. Dr. King gave his life for garbage workers in Memphis, and like Esther, you, Mr. President, were born 'for such a time as this.' You will leave no child or adult behind, because I don't play favorites. Remind them that presidents and world leaders are born both from pedigrees and mixed breeds, and miracles can come out of a mess. There is only one who is spotless; all should embrace this truth."

The Bible is full of people who were accused both openly and behind their backs of dreaming like a fool. President Obama and Dr. King were in great company with centuries of men and women who were ridiculed, mocked, and taunted, and even with one crucified for his ability to hear from God and take heavenly instruction from the GPS navigation system.

It was crystal clear from the presidential race that racism is alive and sickly embedded in the lives, hearts, families, and legacies of many Americans. It is a stronghold that continues to eat away like a ravenous cancer at the core of this country. The hole in the soul

the audacity of faith

of America is destroying the healthy cells, and the poison must be cut out in this generation. If not addressed, the lethal contamination of racism, sexism, and classism will erode this great and glorious land of the "desiring to be free."

President Obama's blackness gives the country an opportunity to expose the cancer of racism and address it at the source. Many seemed not to be ready for a brown-hued messenger, but could it be that this was God's appointed time? Would this great United States of America turn down an exodus from home foreclosures and job losses over a suntan that never goes away?

God does not wait for you or me to catch up to the heavenly plan before execution begins. A dreamer is identified, as in the stories of Joseph in the book of Genesis, Dr. King, and President Obama. It is the dreamer's task to keep his or her eyes always on the Conductor and follow his or her lead.

The world being ready for change is never God's barometer for "Lights, cameras, action." Dr. King might still be in the Birmingham jail, President Obama could still be facilitating focus groups, getting false negative results from well-intentioned citizens, and surely Jesus never would have left his cushioned seat in glory if people's receptivity was the measuring stick for God taking action.

Jesus gave a whole new meaning to winning. He won and he was crucified. People challenged Dr. King, urging him to "wake up and smell the coffee" and pick up the power of guns and weapons to fight against hydrants and hoses being used as weapons of death and destruction. But his Master Teacher, Jesus, and Gandhi, a Hindu brother, showed him a more excellent way.

We have a bad habit of killing dreamers. They seem to stir up our own insecurities, tapping and touching without even knowing they are opening up our "not good enough" wound. Therefore we set out to kill the messenger who exposes continual racism, sexism, and classism. Dreamers adjust the mirror that we rigged to make us look good no matter how bad we look. They display our own warped distortions of our goodness, and we hate them for taking away the veil of our phony goodness and goodwill to all people.

We see how selfish and self-serving we are, how self-absorbed and small-minded our erudite world truly is. We see that we believe more in separate and unequal than in a playing field where everyone gets the rule book to the game.

Those who have been playing longer or have had time to memorize the correct rules should sit out while the others catch up and take their long overdue turn. Or better yet, those with experience and expertise should assist those who have been left behind in catching up, so that the playing field is finally fair and level.

The ultimate one who was thought to be dreaming like a fool was Jesus. Yes, dream, dream, dream like Jesus, who left the comfort of his heavenly abode because he had a dream. He was the dream. He fulfilled the dream to pay a ransom for all, seamlessly reconnecting humanity with God.

Jesus was bruised, mocked, beaten, teased, taunted, bullied, and ultimately crucified. Those who thought that he was dreaming like a fool said, "If you are the Messiah, then save yourself, or call your legions of angels to rescue you." Jesus never addressed his accusers and his abusers. His sacred deathbed conversation was all that mattered. He didn't waste his time or what energy he had left in the wrong places with the wrong people. When the heat was on and time was winding down, Jesus left a very useful example to President Obama, Dr. King, and all other "dreaming fools." That is, don't address absurdity when people are hungry, losing their homes, and in need of help. Don't get sidetracked from the mission.

Let people say that you are dreaming like a fool. Be that fool who knows that with God all things are possible. Be that fool who knows that where two or three are gathered in God's name, God shows up. Be that fool who is certain that "He who began a good work in you will be faithful to complete it." Join the train of "fools" from that great cloud of witnesses mentioned in Hebrews 11 where God made the impossible possible. "For time would fail me to tell you" of all of those for whom God came through, those who were said to be dreaming like a fool.

6
ON THE BORDER OF THE IMPOSSIBLE

GARDNER C. TAYLOR

For many of us the election of Barack Obama to the office of president of the United States of America, also making him the de facto leader of the free world, lies almost on the border of the impossible. This could not be without that Hand in history that is often half hidden—and that belongs to the One who is "from everlasting to everlasting. Amen and Amen" (Psalm 41:13).

The confluence of circumstances surrounding Barack Obama's ascendancy to the White House is nothing short of startling. Just to list the circumstances is breathtaking. They include the marital indiscretions of one of Obama's opponents for a seat in the United States Senate from Illinois, himself a wealthy Harvard graduate without the substantial disadvantage of color. They also include the grim national misadventure in Iraq, the near collapse of the American economic system, and the agonizingly slow maturation of a nation toward its own self-declared political doctrines of equality and opportunity for all persons.

Another surprising confluence of circumstances involved the Republican candidacy for the presidency of a war hero named John McCain who could not disentangle himself from the tragically failed presidency of George W. Bush. Then there was Obama's own emergence as an extraordinarily attractive candidate of color minus the baggage of growing up in those sections of the United States that are mired in centuries-long patterns of injustice and exclusion based solely on skin color. Who could have imagined that America's first black president would emerge from Hawaii and not Harlem?

However, the absence of any firsthand exposure to those American forms of racism that most black people experience from their birth was offset by Obama's apprenticeship on the meaning of blackness in America in one of the nation's most vibrant congregations of color, Trinity United Church of Christ in Chicago, and under the tutelage of Jeremiah Wright, a black pastor with all of the credentials of fearless advocacy together with a profound Christian conviction.

Consider the Obama story on a more personal level. There is his marriage partner, Michelle, a woman of amazing grace and attractiveness with her own impeccable academic credentials. There are their two daughters, Sasha and Malia, children of incandescent loveliness. Finally there is Barack Obama himself, a candidate of charisma and electrifying oratorical skill, joined together with clarity of mind and purpose. Now consider that all of this was joined to a people who were culturally and physically slaughtered but would not die! Their continued existence in the face of harsh oppression was in large measure due to the heralds of hope in every generation since their arrival on American soil asserting that "a better day is coming."

Now, the end result and the startling revelation of "what God hath wrought"—President Barack Obama!

the audacity of faith

7
THIS INAUGURATION:
An Impossible Possibility

JOE KUTTER

What an amazing day it was! It wasn't so many years ago that Rosa Parks was arrested for refusing to give up her seat in the back of the bus so a white man could sit down. On January 20, 2009, we saw Barack and Michelle Obama receive the keys to the White House. And, speaking of transportation, have you seen the brand-new presidential Cadillac? When Rosa Parks refused to give up her seat on the bus, thousands of black people in Montgomery walked to work and back home. Today President Obama is flying in style on Air Force One. Who would have believed it?

From the Emancipation Proclamation to the election of Mr. Obama in fewer than 150 years, as the old cigarette commercial used to say, "You've come a long way, baby." From the marches of Martin Luther King Jr. to this inauguration in fewer than fifty years is a journey of monumental proportion.

The tragedy, of course, is that we had to make this journey at all. If there was ever a testimony to the ability of a people to express both the highest of human aspirations and the lowest of human behaviors it is the story of the American people. In the Declaration of Independence, our forbearers declared, "We hold these truths to be self-evident, that all men are created equal." Inherent in the Constitution was the principle that all persons were equal before the law. Yet that same Constitution included a provision called the three-fifths clause, which stated that a black person was valued at only three-fifths of the value of a white person, at least as far as taxation and the census were concerned. In agreeing to that, those who wrote and signed the U.S. Constitution declared that slavery was an acceptable part of American life. This essential contradiction between slavery and equality has marked America's struggle for its own soul from the beginning.

Now Barack Obama has been inaugurated to be our president. By what stroke of whose imagination did he become the man of the hour? Consider:

> Having a black father from Kenya
> Having a white mother from Kansas
> Absorbing white culture from his mother and
>   grandparents
> Absorbing black culture by virtue of his skin tone
> Living in Hawaii where Asia meets America, where
>   East meets West
> Attending school for a short time in Indonesia
> Graduating from Harvard, the ultimate school of
>   the American establishment
> And now President Obama has moved from working
>   in the depths of the South Side of Chicago with all
>   of its penury to living in the White House with
>   all of its privilege.

Who dreamed up that story?

If it were not happening, you might think it impossible. The odds are all against it, but here we are. To steal and misuse Niebuhr's phrase, we have here an impossible possibility. I have to tell you that even though I am a Christian preacher, I have always been cautious about attributing such things to God. But this sounds like a story that God might write in the pages of human history. As a story of improbability, it fits right in there with Abraham and Sarah, with Moses and Rahab, and with Zechariah and Elizabeth. Our God is a God of improbable stories, and it seems that we have one here.

Before we go too far, let me quickly say that I do not believe that we have been blessed with another Messiah. Somewhere online, I saw an image of DaVinci's *Last Supper*. The faces of all of the disciples had been marked out by question marks, and on top of the Jesus figure sat the face of Barack Obama. I don't know if it was an effort at humor or a mockery of elevated expectations. I will just say that God gave us one Messiah, and that is enough.

Nor do I believe that this election marks the end of racism in America. Racism doesn't go away that easily. Instead, it goes underground, where it hibernates until the circumstances are right to stir it to life again. The pages of history are clear that demagogues are always willing to use the fear of differences as an evil instrument in their quest for power. Witness Hitler in Germany, the tribal conflicts in the Balkans, and the tribal struggles in Iraq for fresh proof of that fact. Racism will never completely go away.

The good news of Obama's election is that racism has in large measure been driven underground. While still alive, it has been weakened, and that is a good thing. It appears that we have in Obama a man who has indeed been judged, in the words of King, "not by the color of his skin, but by the content of his character." That is a benchmark of monumental proportions in American history.

Mr. Obama has been elected as president, the leader of our government, and in that role he becomes the steward of enormous power and responsibility. So, what is the nature of his responsibility? Let me offer some observations. First, government is essential to our humanity. We thrive as individuals only when we live in community. We thrive only as we are organized for the purposes of security, education, and the distribution of resources essential to our well-being. Without government, anarchy would quickly destroy human existence as we know it. Barack Obama is becoming the principal steward of an institution that is essential to the quality of our humanity. He has a huge responsibility and opportunity.

Second, government is always both a reflection and an amplification of human nature. In his little classic *Children of Light and Children of Darkness*, Reinhold Niebuhr said: "Man's capacity for good makes democracy possible. Man's capacity for evil makes democracy necessary." Because government is always the embodiment both of the possibility for good and the potential for evil, it will never be the agency for the arrival of God's kingdom on earth. Even as president of the United States, Mr. Obama will not bring in the kingdom.

When government is good, it accomplishes things we can never do alone, and when it is bad, the evil it can accomplish is multiplied a zillion times over. No single soul could ever create the nuclear energy that provides the electricity that lights our cities. And no individual could ever invent the nuclear bomb that could destroy those same cities. A solitary person kills with a knife or a gun or maybe even a bomb. But governments wage war. A single soul can educate a person or a class, but only governments can build systems of public education. That is why government is both very essential and very dangerous. We must have it, but we must control it.

Mr. Obama is our primary steward of the power of government. He is not our *only* steward of power, thank God. In America, political power is divided and distributed in many different ways—in "checks and balances." But he is our most visible steward, the one who does more than any other to set the tone for the exercise of power.

Government's first job is justice. Many would say that government's first responsibility is security or defense. Government's first job is to protect the people, they say. I would never quarrel about the necessity of defense or security, but that is never enough. In the words of Scripture, the role of government is to protect the "orphan and the widow." Government's role is always to prevent the bully from taking advantage of the weaker neighbor, whether it is on the playground or in the corporate boardroom.

I believe there can be no justice without security. I also know that it is possible to defend the homeland from outside forces while refusing to protect our weaker neighbors from internal bullies. In recent years we have tried to protect ourselves from foreign terrorists, but we have allowed America's financial predators to destroy our national economy. While attempting to providing security against outside attacks, we have nearly self-destructed from the inside precisely because we have ignored the mandate for justice. King said it well. "The arc of the universe is long, but it bends towards justice." Justice is the primary purpose of government.

the audacity of faith

As a Christian I would describe justice this way: justice is the provision of an environment within which every child of God has an opportunity to live the life that God intends for her or him to have. And what is required for the God-intended life? Certainly every child needs the basics of safety, shelter, nutrition, health, education, and opportunity. When a society has the ability to make those necessities available and refuses to do so, justice has been denied—indeed, the very purpose of government has been distorted. Too often we have refused to take care of the widow and orphan.

Mr. Obama is now our primary steward of government's responsibility for justice. As I have listened to him campaign and as I have read his writing, I believe that he understands this first and last responsibility for justice. In saying that, let me retreat to another of Niebuhr's insights. In this world, justice is never fully achievable. Human sin and human limitation, (*finitude*, I believe Niebuhr called it), will always get in the way. But we can always do better. We can more closely approximate justice, we can make it better, and that is our God-given responsibility.

The challenge is, of course, complicated by the realities of the world in which we live. The wars in which we are now engaged make the pursuit of justice more difficult. The global recession that threatens the well-being of millions of persons is making the pursuit of justice harder. The current challenges, both national and international, will provide fresh opportunities for the purveyors of fear and the practitioners of demagoguery to practice their craft.

Even so, I believe that we are standing in a new place, looking toward a new day. We have a new opportunity and the most improbable of stories to tell about a biracial, multicultural man from the western edge of the country who rose to lead us in the quest for justice. He is not the Messiah. We already have one Messiah, and we don't need another. What we need is a president who is committed to justice. Mr. Obama has a remarkable opportunity to respond to God's call for us to fulfill the words of the prophet that "justice will roll down like waters, and righteousness like an everflowing stream" (Amos 5:24). Let it be so, and may God bless Barack Obama, his family, and the United States of America. Amen.

8
A GIANT STEP FORWARD FOR AMERICA

KEN FONG

Americans like to say that in this country anyone can grow up to be president. Until November 4, 2008, that was inarguably true—as long as you were born white and male. Today a forty-seven-year-old African American who was born when someone like himself would have had trouble voting in many parts of the country, and when interracial marriage was illegal in twenty-two states, is president of the United States of America.

> [Obama's] improbable personal journey is inextricably intertwined with the nation's long, bloody road to racial equality. Before it was changed by the Fourteenth Amendment, the Constitution defined someone like Obama as three-fifths of a person. It took the Civil War to end the abomination of slavery, and another century for the civil rights movement to prevail. Obama's victory hardly marks the end of America's most corrosive social affliction, but if racial prejudice and mistrust die in a thousand moments of progress, this is the most important one in a long, long time.[1]

Now that Obama has been elected to be our nation's leader, it is time to put aside partisan-driven ideologies and differences, at least long enough to celebrate what has happened to us as a country. Even if you disagree with all or most of Obama's plans and programs, even if somehow you're still convinced he's a covert Muslim who nevertheless attended a Christian church as a baptized mem-

the audacity of faith

ber for twenty years, you should rejoice as an American that a thick, previously impenetrable glass ceiling has been broken that must have God smiling down on us.

Obama's victory is a moral victory for our country, one that Dr. Martin Luther King Jr. prophesied forty years ago, but which an assassin's bullet kept him from experiencing. If he were still alive, he would have been eighty at the time of Obama's inauguration. I believe he would have emphasized that Obama was elected foremost because Americans deemed him most qualified to lead, and not simply because he was black. Still, of the 95 percent of African Americans who voted for Barack Obama, no doubt many did so primarily because it was their first opportunity to cast a ballot for a black person who actually had a chance to win the presidency.

And who can blame them—especially those who suffered through the evils of bigotry and racism in the darkest of times in America? Certainly not me. And the exit polls indicated that numerous whites—especially in the South—voted against him primarily because he wasn't white or because he was black. I have no sympathy for those people. Clearly we still have a ways to go to embody the principles put in place by the imperfect but prescient founders of this nation.

If you're a follower of Christ—regardless of your political affiliation—I hope that you can appreciate that America's choice of an African American, albeit a biracial one, albeit one who worked long and hard to prove that he was not a threat to white Americans, albeit one who had to distance himself from his "radical" pastor, is a sign of God's justice and not merely the victory of one party over another. For those of us who claim to look at history through redemptive lenses, Obama's election was a breakthrough that some thought would never come. For those of us who are committed to pursuing biblical reconciliation, this was a victory for God's coming kingdom.

Moses led the people of God for forty years of wandering in the desert. When they finally got to the Promised Land, God kept Moses from going in with his people. Nevertheless, he died knowing that they had gotten to where God had pointed them. Forty years ago Dr. King reminded our nation where God had originally pointed us to go, and he, too, never got to see us take those first steps into the Promised Land. Gen. Colin Powell became the first African American secretary of state, and Condoleeza Rice followed in his footsteps. Geraldine Ferraro and then Sarah Palin became the first female major party candidates for the office of vice president. Those were just a few of the notable steps we have taken as a nation toward a Promised Land where all people are judged by the content of their character instead of the color of their skin or their gender.

Their efforts pointed us toward a time in this country when there is truly justice and equal opportunity for all. Electing our first non-white president, though, is a giant step into that storied "land of the free and home of the brave." I hope you will join me in thanking God that this time has finally come and in recommitting ourselves to praying for and working for God's justice for all.

NOTE

1. Editorial, *USA Today*, November 5, 2008.

PART II
BARACK OBAMA and Martin Luther King Jr.

9
NO LONGER A DREAM DEFERRED:
Martin Luther King Jr., Barack Obama, and the Search for the Beloved Community

CAROLYN ANN KNIGHT

I like to pride myself on the fact that I was a huge fan of President Barack Obama before he (to use the hip-hop phrase) "blew up." When I heard him speak at the Democratic National Convention in Boston in 2004, the homiletics professor and the preacher in me said, "He has it." At that time I was not certain what the "it" was, but I knew that he possessed the "it" factor. That speech, "We are not the red states, we are not the blue states, we are the United States of America!" went into my personal canon of greatest speeches of all time. Obama's speech on race, given on March 18, 2008, quickly moved into the canon as well. I had read about his election to the *Harvard Law Review* some years earlier and read his moving memoirs *Dreams from My Father*, about his relationship with his mostly absent father, before it became a *New York Times* best seller.

Since his meteoric rise through the political stratosphere, I have immersed myself in all things "Obama." I have devoured countless books and newspaper and magazine articles. I am a wealth of Obama information. His years as a student at Columbia University in New York City coincided with my graduate student years at

Union Theological Seminary right down the street. Many times in recent days I have wondered if I walked past our future president unaware. Over the years, I have had many opportunities to preach at the Trinity United Church of Christ in Chicago. Now I wonder if a future president was ever in the audience on one of those occasions. On a personal level, Obama's birthday is August 4, mine is August 7. He writes with his left hand, and so do I. Needless to say, I was in Denver in August and Washington, DC, in January.

Why is it necessary to share this information here and now? For me the answer is somewhat of a contradiction. As excited as I am to be a living witness (as opposed to being in that great cloud of witnesses whom I believe are aware of these glorious events), as happy and hopeful as I am about the prospects of the Obama presidency, and as proud as I am of this great nation, I am reluctant and hesitant to celebrate the fulfillment of Dr. Martin Luther King Jr.'s dream or our collective and communal arrival at the Promised Land/beloved community.

For the purpose of this writing, I will discuss my reluctance by focusing on two of the questions offered as suggestions for this volume: (1) In what ways does the election of Barack Obama suggest the fulfillment of the words of Martin Luther King Jr. from April 3, 1968, "We as a people will get to the Promised Land"? and (2) What are the biblical and/or theological terms and concepts that you have used as you have reflected on an Obama presidency?

Simply stated, the election of Barack Obama suggests that America has awakened from its long, nightmarish slumber of racial polarization and division to embrace the dawn of what is possible when we move beyond race as a criterion for human involvement in society. This is a bad dream from which we have been trying to rouse ourselves for far too long.

Second, two Scriptures supply the theological language that informs my thinking and hopefulness about the Obama presidency:

> So the scribe said to Him, to love God with all the heart, with all the understanding, with all the soul, and with all the strength, and to love one's neighbor as oneself, is more

than all the whole burnt offerings and sacrifices. Now when Jesus saw that he answered wisely, He said to him, "You are not far from the kingdom of God." (Mark 12:32-34 NKJV).

I saw a new heaven and a new earth, for the first heaven and the first earth had passed away. (Revelation 22:1 NKJV).

There is indeed a new earth and a new world order emerging, but we have much to do. So I want to offer the Obama presidency as another, although significant vehicle that will move us further along on our journey toward the beloved community.

Perhaps the profoundest theme that runs throughout the sermons and speeches of Martin Luther King Jr. is the concept of the beloved community. The vision of this community, the full inclusion of humanity into a totally integrated society, began to unfold during King's student days at Crozer Theological Seminary in Chester, Pennsylvania. It continued on through his pastoral work in Montgomery and Atlanta, and culminated during his civil rights activism with the Southern Christian Leadership Conference.

King's intellectual pilgrimage can best be described as follows: liberalism and personalism provided the theological and philosophical foundations of the concept; nonviolence provided the means to attain it; the Christian realism of Reinhold Niebuhr qualified King's initial optimism about the possibility of actualizing it within history and changed King's attitude about the kinds of tactics necessary to move toward it.[1]

King's understanding of the beloved community was a holistic inclusion of humanity into a moral, political, economic, and spiritual fabric woven together through the forces of agape love. Unlike desegregation, it could not be legislated. For King the realization of the beloved community and the realization of the dream were a matter of head and heart. Desegregation was important but insufficient when it came to his vision for America. The realization of the beloved community required more.

For King the journey toward the beloved community would require that whites and blacks begin to see each other through different eyes and learn to treat each other in more humane ways. Whites would have to see blacks as fully human, and blacks would have to learn to see whites as capable of being loving and compassionate human beings. Together both groups would have to understand the United States as a shared universe where "black and white" could live together block by block and neighborhood by neighborhood.

This model could not be legislated or voted into reality. This type of change in attitude and spirit would come into being only as blacks and whites began to live, work, and play together in community. When segregation has been abolished and desegregation has been accomplished, blacks and whites will have to learn to relate to each other across those nonrational psychological barriers that have traditionally separated them in our society.[2]

The greatest visual that we have had in recent history of the beloved community is what is now being called the Barack Obama era. Unlike anyone in recent history, and perhaps even more effectively than King himself, Obama has been able to form a human coalition of blacks and whites, females and males, young and old, religious and secular, persons of all gender persuasions and all economic and educational ranks who believe in a singular theme—that we can make the world better for ourselves and for the next generation.

Obama was uniquely qualified to inherit the mantle of Martin Luther King Jr. because of his own diverse family heritage: "I am the son of a father from Kenya and a white mother from Kansas." His search for self-awareness and identity drove Obama to become an ardent student of the African American context, and in doing so he "came to himself." Sounding like the African American preachers that influenced him in Chicago, Obama took to the political pulpit to convert all Americans to his message of a changed humanity.

In the same way that we believed the message of King, we believe the message of Obama. I have always believed that the greatest testament to anyone's preaching is that persons who hear the sermon do what the preacher tells them to do. When King preached, people marched. When Obama spoke, we became a human mosaic determined to live together and to be better together.

Yet Obama will admit that we have many difficult days ahead. The world is so much different than it was in 1968 when Dr. King was assassinated. The United States has to learn to work together within the new landscape of diversity, multiculturalism, and pluralism at home as well as abroad. Wars and rumors of war are an ever-present reality. Corporate greed and economic mismanagement have brought global economic markets to virtual collapse. The world's ecological and environmental systems are in peril. The list goes on and on and on. So even though we have moved farther along in our journey toward the Promised Land, we are still very much a people on the way, a work in progress.

To be sure, there has not been much to celebrate in recent days. There are too many young lives that should be here to see this new America, but they are no longer with us. They gave their lives on the battlefields of Iraq and Afghanistan. They, too, made this time possible. We can never forget them. We owe them a great debt. They must always be celebrated for their role in advancing the realization of the global beloved community.

President Obama has already signed into law the equal pay for equal work bill, guaranteeing that women will now receive the same pay for doing the same work as men. Now, if only the Christian church would embrace the notion of equality in the pulpit, we would be moving even closer to the beloved community. To be sure, there is work to be done. We will always be challenged to navigate the sometimes tumultuous terrain of race, gender, and class. But I believe that there is a renewed spirit in all of us as we continue this journey.

While the articulation of the beloved community can be done by one voice such as King or Obama, it takes the whole community, flawed and fragmented as we are, to bring the dream to fulfillment. It takes our collective will to work for change. Just as Dr. King envisioned that massive crowd that gathered at the Lincoln Memorial on August 28, 1963, as the ones who would usher in the beloved community, President Obama will need that great sea of humanity that gathered in Washington, DC, on January 20, 2009, to be champions for the cause of real change in America.

I was a child when Dr. King articulated his dream for America. I was a teenager when he envisioned his hope of the American Promised Land. I am now a fully grown woman who always believed that this day would come. So compellingly were the words of Martin Luther King when I heard them that I believed them and had hope in them. His words allowed me to believe in a fully integrated society. When I heard them, I always believed that I would see an African American elected to the highest office in the land in my lifetime. I know this is contrary to many who thought they would never see it, but I believed in Martin Luther King, I believe in Barack Obama, and I believe God.

Crea en Dios! Believe in God!

NOTES

1. Kenneth L. Smith and Ira G. Zepp Jr., *Search for the Beloved Community: The Thinking of Martin Luther King Jr.* (Valley Forge, PA: Judson, 1998), 129.

2. Ibid., 131.

the audacity of faith

10
WHEN THE WALLS CAME TUMBLING DOWN

MARVIN A. McMICKLE

The election of Barack Obama as the forty-fourth president of the United States of America brought to my mind the lyrics "Joshua fit the battle of Jericho, and the walls came tumbling down." That song dates back to the era of slavery in the United States, but it points back to one of the earliest stories in the Bible. Moses sent out twelve spies to view the Promised Land and bring back a report on the defenses of that city. While ten spies said the city could not be conquered, there were two spies, Joshua and Caleb, who said it was possible.

The conquest of Jericho was not something that the majority of the people of Israel expected to see. They believed those walls would stand between them and their Promised Land. In fact, after the ten spies delivered their report, the people told Moses that they should either have stayed in Egypt or died in the desert, rather than come to this walled city they were unable to conquer. Despite the broad negative sentiment, two of those spies believed that the walls could be brought down, and that is exactly what happened in Joshua 6. The great walled city of Jericho was conquered. Its enormous walls came "tumbling down."

There are several significant parallels between the walls of Jericho and some other walls that came tumbling down in the United States when Barack Obama was elected to be the U.S. president. The first parallel pays homage to earlier generations of people who did not live to see their people enter into the Promised Land. In Deuteronomy 32 God allowed Moses to climb to the top of Mount Nebo, and from that vantage point he was able to see the Promised Land. He saw it, but he was not able to enter into that land. On April 3, 1968, Dr. Martin Luther King Jr. told a crowd in Memphis that God had allowed him to go to the mountaintop, and he had looked over. He said, "I've seen the Promised Land." Then he told that crowd, "I may not get there with you, but I want you to know tonight that we as a people will get to the Promised Land."

In what was surely one of the most dramatic and transformative days in American history, it felt to many people as if they had entered the Promised Land when Barack Obama became president. However, the leaders and laborers of an earlier generation did not live to enjoy that day; it was the leaders and laborers of the next generation who led the way into our future as a people and as a nation. There were some people, such as Congressman John Lewis and Dorothy Height, who did make the full journey from the hard struggles of the 1960s to actually being there to see Obama sworn in as president. The powerful benediction offered by Joseph Lowery served as a lyrical bridge that spanned from the earlier generations of black Americans who struggled and died on their way to freedom to those millions who packed the National Mall to see with their own eyes the making of history with Obama's election. But on the whole, the election of the nation's first black president was a dream that while fed and nurtured by an earlier generation, was not fulfilled in their lifetime.

Make no mistake about it; Obama's election was not the singular success of this obviously gifted and talented individual. His election was a significant step in a journey that began in the eighteenth and nineteenth century when black slaves starting running for freedom, when sharecroppers wanted to own the land they worked, when people in Montgomery decided to walk in dignity rather than ride in segregation. If it had not been for the courage and faith and struggles of many people, most of whose names will never be known, there would not have been a victory for the generation of Joshua to enjoy. The same truth applies today; if it had not been for the people who marched and picketed and died for the right to vote in the 1950s and 1960s, there would be no President Obama today.

the audacity of faith

The second parallel involves the fact that Joshua did not walk around those walls seven times by himself. The text is very clear that all the people of his generation would have to do their part if they wanted to achieve the final victory. Joshua 6:6-8 points out that the priests, the soldiers, and all the people of Israel were told to walk around the walls seven times. The people were not simply to watch and wait while Joshua did all the work; everybody had to do his or her part. The priests had to carry the trumpets and rams' horns and blow at the proper time. The warriors had to walk behind the priests. When the moment came, all the people had to shout together in one great shout. Not just Joshua alone, but all the people caused the walls to come tumbling down.

And it was not just black people who made Obama's victory possible. It took white people in Iowa to convince black people all across America that Obama could win this election. It took three former slave-holding states—North Carolina, Virginia, and Florida—to give this victory to Barack Obama. It took older people willing to stand in line for two and three hours to cast their vote. It took younger people willing to drop out of college or take a leave from their jobs to work full-time for this campaign. It took delegates from all fifty states that paid their own way to go to Denver to nominate Obama at the Democratic National Convention. It took three million people who were willing to support the campaign financially with smaller than usual amounts of money. The walls came tumbling down because, as at Jericho, everybody did his or her part.

Here is the third parallel: notice that the walls of Jericho did not come tumbling down at the end of the first day of walking. The people had to walk around those walls for seven consecutive days before the walls came down. Most things worth having are things for which we have to be willing to work and wait. The world can be a different place; Obama's election points to that fact. Nevertheless, we all have to work and wait for the changes we want to occur.

In his speech on November 4 after he had been elected, Obama said, "This election is not the change that we seek. This election is the chance to make the change that we want to see." With Obama's election we have a chance to be sure that all Americans receive some form of health care, but we will have to work and wait for that change to come. We have a chance to end the wars in Iraq and Afghanistan and to defeat all forms of both domestic and international terrorism, but we have to work and wait for the change we want to see. We have a chance to stimulate the American economy so that it not only benefits major corporations and their middle-class consumers, but so that it also benefits the ones Jesus referred to "as the least of these," the ones who always seem to be forgotten or overlooked when politicians move from campaign mode to the implementation of policies. The country we have been dreaming about since 1776 is finally in sight but not yet completely in reach; everybody from the White House to my house and your house needs to work and wait for the change we want to see!

The next parallel is tied to the observation that while the story about the walls of Jericho tumbling down extends to Joshua 6:21, I end my consideration of this passage with verse 20. Why not go one verse deeper into this story? Because in verse 21 when the people of Israel finally entered the city of Jericho after the walls came tumbling down, they killed every person and every animal in that city except for Rahab the prostitute and her family.

I left that verse out of this sermon because that is not how God wants our 2009 story to end. God wants our story to end very differently, with people all across this country finally coming together to live as neighbors and friends. God may not have wanted the people of Israel to share the city of Jericho with the people who were already living there, but God surely does want us to share this country and this world together. Barack Obama will not name black people to every position in his new administration, and that is okay; God wants us to live in this country together. Of course, many of us had hoped he would have named many more than seems to be the case right now. Nevertheless, we must understand, as did Nelson Mandela and the people of South Africa, that no matter what the people did in the past to help bring the walls down, what we have to do both now and in the future is work for ways to live together now that some of the walls that have long divided us are tumbling down.

The final parallel is a graphic reminder that politics alone and Barack Obama alone cannot get us where we need and want to go. In Joshua 6:6 Joshua told the people, "Take up the ark of the covenant, and have seven priests carry seven trumpets of rams' horns in front of the ark of the LORD." The ark of the covenant represented the presence of God in the midst of the people.

No secular media outlets would share in this view, nor will many Americans who cast their vote on November 4, 2008, but I believe Obama's election was an act of divine intervention; a *kairos* moment when God broke into history as we experience it to advance the agenda of God's kingdom. This "divine interruption" of politics as usual helped move us beyond the bigotries and biases that have hindered our country from reaching its full potential as a nation allegedly rooted in the principle that all people are created equal. The Obama election was an answer to years of prayer, and it was a tangible sign of the active presence of a just God who is still present in the midst of a sinful and unjust world. I believe as Psalm 127 declares, "Unless the LORD builds the house, its builders labor in vain. Unless the LORD watches over the city, the watchmen stand guard in vain" (NIV).

I do not doubt that Barack Obama is both an intelligent and an intuitive political leader; but we will need more than that to overcome the challenges that confront our nation and our planet. I am overjoyed that there is a black man in the White House whose campaign message was "Yes, we can," but my deepest convictions are rooted in the song that says:

> My hope is built on nothing less
> than Jesus' blood and righteousness.
> I dare not trust the sweetest frame,
> but wholly lean on Jesus' name.
> On Christ the solid rock I stand,
> all other ground is sinking sand.

11
ALMOST BUT NOT QUITE

GINA M. STEWART

Well, I don't know what will happen now. We've got some difficult days ahead. But it really doesn't matter with me now, because I've been to the mountaintop. And I don't mind. Like anybody, I would like to live a long life. Longevity has its place. But I'm not concerned about that now. I just want to do God's will. And He's allowed me to go up to the mountain. And I've looked over. And I've seen the Promised Land. I may not get there with you. But I want you to know tonight, that we, as a people, will get to the Promised Land![1]

I was only eight years old when Dr. Martin Luther King Jr. came to Memphis to support sanitation workers in their fight against low wages and inhumane working conditions. Of the events at Mason Temple on the evening of April 3, 1968, when King delivered his last and often quoted speech, Rev. Samuel Billy Kyles, pastor, civil rights leader, and eyewitness to the assassination of King, has often stated, "It was on that evening, marked by active thunderstorms, that an enthusiastic, packed crowd heard Dr. King give what has come to be known as the 'Mountaintop' speech. In it, he gave an unusual glimpse into his personal fears and challenges, as well as his prophetic insights into his own fate. It's as if he preached himself through the fear of death." On the following day, Dr. King was assassinated while standing on the balcony of the Lorraine Motel as he and his entourage were preparing to go to the home of Rev. Kyles for a home-cooked meal.

The words of Dr. King's speech the night before his death recount the experience of Moses, who climbed from the Moabite plain to the summit of Mount Nebo, at the peak of Mount Pisgah, to view the land promised to Israel. Moses, the servant of the Lord, died in the plains of Moab without ever setting a foot in the Promised Land. After directly confronting Pharaoh and navigating an exodus of God's people through uncharted territory, Moses passed the baton to Joshua, son of Nun, who would be the one to lead the Israelites into the land of promise.[2]

On Tuesday, January 20, 2009, the day following the national holiday honoring King, I stood in the crowd of more than one million to watch as Barack Hussein Obama took the oath of office not only as the forty-fourth president of the United States of America, but as the nation's first black president. While many have heralded this moment in time as the realization and fulfillment of King's dream, we must remember that racial equality was only one dimension of King's dream.

The country over which President Obama will preside is drowning in a sea of debt, an "economic tsunami," as so aptly described by Alan Greenspan. Voter registration, voter disenfranchisement, and voter suppression tactics still impact a disproportionate number of minorities. Nearly 36 million people live in poverty; children wake up hungry and go to bed hungry; we have two wars raging; more than 45 million are without health care; our education system needs an overhaul; we live under the threat of nuclear war; and violence, gangs, and guns claim the lives of our young at alarming rates.

While it is important not to minimize the significance of what transpired on January 20, it is also important to resist the temptation to declare that King's dream has been fulfilled.

Lest we forget, it was on April 4, 1967 (just one year prior to his death) when King delivered one of his most controversial statements at a meeting of Clergy and Laity Concerned about Vietnam at the Riverside Church in New York. In his sermon entitled "A Time to Break the Silence," King denounced the American government for its addiction to violence and for its spiritual bankruptcy. He said:

A nation that continues year after year to spend more money on military defense than on programs of social uplift is approaching spiritual death. America, the richest and most powerful nation in the world, can well lead the way in this revolution of values. There is nothing, except a tragic death wish, to prevent us from reordering our priorities, so that the pursuit of peace will take precedence over the pursuit of war. There is nothing to keep us from molding a recalcitrant status quo with bruised hands until we have fashioned it into a brotherhood.[3]

The prophet Isaiah captured the essence of King's challenge to embrace a revolution of values. Isaiah envisioned a redeemed social order. He prophesied about an idyllic setting where the wolf and the lamb, the leopard and the baby goat, the lion and the yearling, and the cow and the bear would live in harmony. Wild beasts and little children would play together near the hole of the cobra and the viper absolutely unafraid, and a little child will lead the beasts (11:6-8). But Isaiah's prophecy sounded unrealistic against the backdrop of exile, oppression, and alienation brought on by the chosen nation's failure to cultivate intimacy with God.

In a society like ours, where people seem bent on destruction, Isaiah's prophecy sounds as unrealistic as King's summons to a worldwide fellowship that lifts neighborly concern beyond one's class, race, and political party. Our nation has not been the same since September 11 or Katrina or the war on terror. Fear of biological warfare, heightened airport security, escalating violence between Israel and Palestine, military confrontations, corrupt politics, corporate greed, mortgage meltdowns, corporate bailouts, and a recession are symptomatic of the times in which we live. More than 11 million people are out of work, and unemployment benefits have reached the highest level in more than forty years. The thought of peaceful coexistence, cooperation, and collaboration seems just as unrealistic for our times as Isaiah's.

Nevertheless, Isaiah prophesied about a societal transformation. He used the imagery of the altered temperament of the animal king-

the audacity of faith

dom to describe the transformed environment that will not be ruled by animal instinct, but by a recognition of the authority of God.

This environment of transformed relationships would be ushered in by a shoot that would come up from the stump of Jesse, a fruit-bearing branch. This fruit-bearing branch would possess impeccable credentials, because he would be filled with the Spirit of God who would administer the affairs of God's kingdom with justice and equity.

Inquiring minds want to know when Isaiah's prophecy and King's dream will be fulfilled. While Obama's presidency represents a partial fulfillment of King's dream for America, we know that Isaiah's prophecy was fulfilled in the person and work of Jesus Christ. Jesus was the stump of Jesse who came as a baby to usher in the kingdom of God, who by the Spirit of the Lord, ruled with wisdom and understanding, counsel and might, knowledge and the fear of the Lord (Isaiah 11:2). Jesus was the fulfillment of Isaiah's prophecy when he gave his life for the sins of the world. Today Jesus is seated at the right hand of God, and according to the Scriptures, Jesus is coming back again.

However, until Jesus returns there will be Osama Bin Ladens and terrorist cells that threaten our safety. Until Jesus returns racism, sexism, and classism will present their own challenges. Until Jesus returns people will struggle with distorted value systems. Until Jesus returns there will be those who choose popularity over principle, image over integrity, success over significance, reputation over character, and convenience over standing by their convictions. Until Jesus returns people will kill and compete with each other. Until Jesus returns lofty ideals will be slaughtered on the battlefield of competition, self-interest, and self-indulgence. Until Jesus returns nations and tribes will continue to squabble.

Now that the euphoria of the inauguration of Obama has passed, will we open our eyes to the unfinished business that lies ahead of us? As comforting as it may be to have a "brother" in the White House, will we be among the ones who choose to sit on the sidelines of history, or will we be counted among the remnant who will help President Obama to pursue a more just and equitable society? Will we continue to work toward creating what theologians call an eschatological present? Will we function as what Dr. Forrest Harris calls "agents of reconstruction," architects of broken dreams who labor to construct an alternate view of reality that is influenced by the reign of God?

In order for that to happen, we must reconcile the wolf and the lamb, the predator and prey inside of us.

- There is a tiger within us that is fierce and blood thirsty for power control and domination.
- There is a wolf inside us that is crafty, covetous, and destructive.
- There is a leopard inside of us that is waiting to pounce upon anything that looks like diversity.
- There a lion in us that likes to bite and devour.
- There is a bear in us that likes to growl and intimidate others.
- There is a cobra in us that is venomous and spiteful and poisonous, calculating and waiting to strike at any moment.

For some this analogy may sound a bit disturbing, for we are not wolves and tigers, lions and bears, vipers and cobras; we are the righteousness of God in Christ Jesus. We are fellow citizens of the household of faith and joint heirs with Jesus Christ.

That's right. Humanity is more than a beast, but it does not take a rocket scientist to see that humanity does not always function like angels. Both the wolf and the lamb are within us. We are indeed a bundle of contrasts! What shall we do with ourselves, with this bundle of contradictions, with this combination of wolf and lamb?

It is only through yielding ourselves to Jesus Christ that we can be fundamentally changed. When we repent of sin and claim Jesus Christ as Savior and Lord, his Holy Spirit begins to restrain the beast within us and unleash the angel.

When the beast within is restrained, and the angel is unleashed, we become messengers who have fellowship with God and carry out God's will. We become Jesus' advance troops. We become mediators who proclaim God's will and live the reign of God. We become empowered to influence the world's transformation. We become repairers of the breach and restorers of streets. We become trumpet blowers for justice, righteousness, equality, and inclusivity.

When the angel is released we speed up that great day Martin talked about and Isaiah dreamed about, when every valley shall be exalted and every crooked place shall be made straight and all flesh shall see it together. For the mouth of the Lord has spoken it. The entire earth will be filled with the knowledge of the Lord. Hallelujah! Amen!

NOTES

1. James Washington, ed., *I Have a Dream: Writings and Speeches That Changed the World* (San Francisco: HarperSanFrancisco, 1986), 203.

2. See Deuteronomy 34:1-9.

3. Washington, *I Have a Dream*, 148–49.

12
WORKING FROM THE BOTTOM UP

PHILIP YANCEY

On November 4, 2008, I boarded a plane just before polling places closed on the East Coast. Stepping off the plane three hours later, I asked the first person I saw, an African American baggage handler, "Do you know who won the election?" He proceeded to give me a complete breakdown of the electoral college results and which states Barack Obama would need to clinch victory. I got a strong clue as to how much this election means to a people who have spent far more years oppressed than liberated by democracy.

The next day I toured the Civil Rights Museum built around the Lorraine Motel where Martin Luther King Jr. was assassinated in 1968. For several hours I revisited the scenes I had known so well as a teenager coming of age in the South. The brave college students in Greensboro, North Carolina, who in 1960 sat at a lunch counter as goons stamped out cigarettes in their hair, squirted mustard and ketchup in their faces, then knocked them off the stools and kicked them while white policemen looked on, laughing. The eerie scenes of weightless children flying through mist in Birmingham, propelled by high-powered fire hoses directed at them by city officials. The Freedom Riders' bus burned in Alabama, the corpses unburied in Mississippi.

Looking back, it seems incredible to imagine such ferocity directed against people who were seeking the basic ingredients of human dignity: the right to vote, the right to eat in restaurants and stay in motels, the right to attend college (two hundred National Guard troops escorted James Meredith to his first class, and even so, people died in the ensuing riots).

Outside the museum, words from King's final "I have been to the mountaintop" speech are forged in steel. They are words that caught in my throat on a sunny day mere hours after Barack Obama got elected: "I may not get there with you, but I want you to know that we, as a people, will get to the Promised Land." The very next day after King said these words, he died in a pool of blood on the exact spot where I was standing.

In no way do I discount the important policy differences between Obama and many Christians. But, at the least, can we use this moment as a time of reflection and, yes, repentance over our share in the sin of racism that has marked this nation since its founding? It took Southern Baptists 150 years to apologize for their support of slavery, and not until late 2008 did Bob Jones University admit their error in barring black students before 1971. Their words of apology—"We failed to accurately represent the Lord and to fulfill the commandment to love others as ourselves"—apply to many of us, for many Christians vigorously opposed the civil rights movement. Can we now respond to a leader's call for racial healing and reconciliation?

During the campaign I received scurrilous e-mails about Obama, pointing out that he was a child of Africa, "The dark continent where worship of demonic spirits, bloodshed, and violence have been the rule"; a child of Islam, "a religion based upon absolute submission to the god of forces and violence for all infidels"; and "a well-documented deceiver/liar who's [sic] tongue is set on fire with the flames of hell." How far have we come, after all?

Two weeks after the election, I traveled to India where I met Christian pioneers who are seeking to overturn India's institutional form of racism, the caste system. One scholar said to me, "You Americans are celebrating the election of a black man only 250 years after slavery. We are still waiting for liberation after 4,000 years of living under caste." The Dalit Freedom Network works on behalf of 160 million Dalits, formerly known as "untouchables." Though nominally Hindu, Dalits are not even allowed in Hindu temples and in recent years have increasingly turned to other religions, including Christianity. Just above them are the "other backward castes," 600 million strong, who comprise more than half of India's population. An organization called Truthseekers spearheads efforts on their behalf. The activists coming out of these castes see Hinduism as an oppressive social structure, designed to keep them "in their place." Any sign of agitation prompts a response, often violent, from fundamentalist Hindus who want to maintain the status quo.

Joseph D'Souza, president of the All India Christian Council, said, "Early missionaries directed their efforts toward the Brahmins, the upper castes, hoping the liberating message of the Gospel would trickle down to the oppressed. It didn't happen. Now we are working from the bottom up." As he described the history of Christianity in India, I could not help thinking of parallels in my own country. Some evangelicals are wringing their hands over their loss of access to the corridors of power. Maybe it's time for us, too, to work from the bottom up.

13

OF DREAMS AND THEIR DREAMERS:
A Sermonic Reflection of the Significance of the Obama Presidency

WIL GAFNEY

"They said to one another, "Look! This master dreamer is coming. Now, let us kill him...and we shall see what will become of his dreams."[1]

A version of this abbreviated text from Genesis 37:19-20, drawn from the Joseph story, is engraved on the marker memorializing the martyrdom of the Rev. Dr. Martin Luther King Jr. in Memphis on the balcony of the Lorraine Hotel where he was murdered. In this year, which would have marked Dr. King's eightieth birthday, a year highlighted by the inauguration of this nation's first president of African descent, many are asking if Dr. King's dream has been fulfilled. I would like to suggest that even as we celebrate the inauguration of our forty-fourth president, Barack Hussein Obama, that Dr. King's dream has not yet been fulfilled in totality.

Let us pray: *"God of dreams and dreamers, hear the cries of your people, cries of acclamation and celebration, and cries for compassion, consolation, and a continuation of reconciliation and transformation in this world. Amen."*

Consider the words of Dr. King's "I have a dream" speech, delivered in 1963 on the steps of the memorial to President Abraham Lincoln, whose bicentennial birthday our nation and our president, himself also a former senator from Illinois, celebrate on the heels of Dr. King's birthday and President Obama's inauguration. What has become of the dreams of the master dreamer?

> I have a dream that my four little children will one day live in a nation where they will not be judged by the color of their skin but by the content of their character. I have a dream today!
>
> I have a dream that one day, down in Alabama, with its vicious racists, with its governor having his lips dripping with the words of "interposition" and "nullification"— one day right there in Alabama little black boys and black girls will be able to join hands with little white boys and white girls as sisters and brothers.[2]

There are many places in this nation, including the Deep South, where children of every race, color, creed, nationality, and ethnicity are free to play together. However, there are also many places in this nation—north and south, east and west—and across this whole wide world, where women and men and boys and girls are not judged by the content of their character, but by some external marker, including: skin color, gender, place of origin, immigration status, sexual orientation, or socioeconomic status.

Consider those interpersonal, interethnic, and international hatreds of all sorts, including but not limited to those atrocities that our government designates as hate crimes. Consider those hate crimes that we will not call such—rape, genocide, ethnic cleansing. These all demonstrate with a terrible power that Dr. King's dream has yet to be fulfilled for all of us, despite the remarkable accomplishments of President Obama and many, many others in the public and private sectors.

> *"Let the prophet who has a dream tell the dream."*
> (Jeremiah 23:28)

When I think of Dr. King's dream, I turn to two other messages he left us. One is the sermon Dr. King preached at the Riverside

the audacity of faith

Church in New York City on April 4, 1967, exactly one year to the day before his martyrdom. The other is the sermon that he preached on April 3, 1968, at Mason Temple in Memphis, on the night before his translation from life to life. In these two sermons, the prophet-dreamer revealed how long is the road we must travel before we as a nation can proclaim, "Mission accomplished!"

In his Riverside sermon, Dr. King scandalized many in this nation, black and white alike, by identifying war as a civil and human rights issue. He was deeply saddened to encounter people who claimed not to know that peace and civil rights *do* mix. In that sermon, Dr. King prophesied against the dismantling of antipoverty programs to construct the engines of war. His oracle endures today: "I knew that America would never invest the necessary funds or energies in rehabilitation of its poor so long as adventures like Vietnam continue to draw men and skills and money like some demonic destructive suction tube."[3]

As I reflect on these words today, our nation and our world seem to have been driven to the brink of bankruptcy by a global economic collapse. At the same time that our nation's power brokers are fostering policies that many around the world fault for our common calamity, our nation is spending billions of dollars, offering up the bodies of thousands of women and men, and squandering the energies and skills of international coalitions to wage war, to tear down, to destroy—allegedly, in order to build.

Our nation's response to its own fiscal irresponsibility and instability is to pour more than a trillion dollars into financial institutions without requiring them to lend one red cent to the suffering and struggling people of this nation. Lawmakers who did not argue about how much money to give to banking and insurance agencies, or on how quickly to give it, are now heard arguing about whether to permit states to relieve the suffering of their people with job-producing projects funded by Obama's recently adopted economic stimulus plan.

I invite you to look up the words of the prophetic Riverside sermon, particularly the section about how the United States of

America must have appeared as "strange liberators" to the Vietnamese people, and imagine how these words might sound to the people of Iraq and Afghanistan today. One aspect of Dr. King's dream that I believe has yet to be fulfilled is his call for specific action by this nation's citizens to end the unjust practices of our government here and around the world. He lays out some of these in his Riverside sermon, as well as in his prescient "Mountaintop" sermon 364 days later at Mason Temple on the eve of his assassination.

In Memphis, the former stronghold of southern-fried chattel slavery, reconfigured and reversed Reconstruction, Jim and Jane Crow, and old-fashioned American-style racism, Dr. King called for black folk to put their collective financial power to work on behalf of all the poor people of this nation and around the world including the American North with its white supremacist ideologies. He called specifically for the boycott of Coca-Cola, Wonder Bread, and Hart's Bread. He challenged all African American families and businesses to divest themselves of insurance policies and bank accounts with dominant culture firms that discriminated against black people, and that mistreated poor people of every ethnicity.

> *...the dream is certain, and its interpretation is faithful.*
> (Daniel 2:45)

Dr. King understood that the global economy thrives on the broken bodies and dashed dreams of the poor of this world, most of whom are people of color. He once said, "If something isn't done, and in a hurry, to bring the colored peoples of the world out of their long years of poverty, ...their long years of hurt and neglect, the whole world is doomed."[4] Dr. King understood what Langston Hughes had in mind when he said that a dream deferred does not always dry up like a raisin in the sun; sometimes it *explodes*.

> *And they hated him even more because of his dreams and his words.* (Genesis 37:8)

The once detested dreamer has become an American saint whose gospel of nonviolent social revolution has swept the globe. I believe that Dr. King is rejoicing in his choir loft in heaven, sharing in the communion of saints, in part because a sun-kissed son of Africa has been elected the leader of the United States and therefore of the free world. We can expect more from this administration, because President Obama's campaign prioritized the concerns of people of all colors, ethnicities, and religions, as well as policies and priorities that include the amelioration and eradication of poverty.

The dreamer King dreamed of hope and transformation. He now lives in that land where he has no need of dreams. Our need for dreams, however, continues day by day. We are a nation of dreamers; indeed, the whole world is full of dreamers. There are more than 230 million dreamers in this nation, and there are 2 billion people all across our fragile globe who want to be able to feed themselves and their children; care for their elders; trust that when they need medical care that it will be available to them; pursue meaningful work; and live, love, and laugh in peace and stability. And more dreamers are born every day.

> And it will be so that afterward
> I will pour out my spirit on all flesh;
> your sons and your daughters shall prophesy,
> your old men shall dream dreams,
> and your young men shall see visions.
> —Joel 2:28

Amen.

NOTES
1. All Scripture references are the translations of the author.
2. Ibid., 232–33.
3. Ibid., 280.

14
A LIFTING OF THE BURDEN[1]

CURTISS PAUL DeYOUNG

In his book *The Luminous Darkness* (Harper, 1965), Howard Thurman wrote that "the burden of being black and the burden of being white is so heavy that it is rare in our society to experience oneself as a human being." The election of Barack Obama as the forty-fourth president of the United States lifted that burden for many African Americans and other persons of color. Even if it lifted only for a few hours or a few days, it was a welcome experience. Many whites went to the polls and cast a vote based on the content of their candidate's character. They did not allow the color of his skin to sway their decision. These whites also felt the burden lift, even if only for a short time. The election of Barack Obama was a powerful moment of reconciliation. After five centuries of racial injustice in America, millions of people reclaimed a greater sense of their humanity. The question then, at the commencement of an Obama presidency, is this: Can the moment become a season of reconciliation? And can a season of reconciliation cause a permanent shift toward a less racist and more reconciled society?

There have been moments in U.S. history when a national breakthrough for reconciliation seemed near. In 1968 the multiracial coalitions formed by the Poor People's Campaign of Martin Luther King Jr. and the political campaign of Robert F. Kennedy had great promise. Yet these coalitions did not cause a shift on the landscape of reconciliation. Forty years later the United States is in the midst of a dramatic demographic shift. At the midpoint of the twenty-first century the United States will be a culturally diverse and pluralistic nation with no racial majority.

the audacity of faith

The population will be 46 percent white, 30 percent Latino, 15 percent black or African, 9 percent Asian, and the remainder Native Americans, multiracial people, and others (U.S. Census Bureau). The diverse movement that coalesced to elect Barack Obama signaled this new reality. The flexing of political muscle by Latinos in the election was another sign. Can the Obama coalition become the foundation for a shift in racial dynamics in the United States? Time will tell.

Racism and injustice have not ended because one black person was elected president of the United States. The demographic changes that are producing greater cultural diversity may result in increased bigotry and racial tensions. Economic privilege is still overwhelmingly in the hands of whites. Churches remain segregated by race and socioeconomic class. The singular event of an African American ascending to the most powerful position in the world does not automatically translate into greater access to seats of power in corporate, government, and nonprofit entities for persons of color.

Yet the presidency of Barack Obama is a significant step forward in what he called "the long march…for a more just, more equal, more free, more caring and more prosperous America" (March 18, 2008). It lifts the burden that Howard Thurman claimed was so pervasive long enough for folks to stand up straighter and embrace a greater sense of their humanity. In many ways, the election of Barack Obama as president allows us to take a first step into the Promised Land that Martin Luther King Jr. spoke about the day before he was assassinated. In 1968 King proclaimed, "I've seen the Promised Land. I may not get there with you. But I want you to know tonight that we as a people will get to the Promised Land." Forty years later Barack Obama stated on election night, "If there is anyone out there who still doubts that America is a place where all things are possible; who still wonders if the dream of our founders is alive in our time; who still questions the power of democracy, tonight is your answer." While Obama's words may claim that we are further down the road to reconciliation than reality can support, his election is a significant milestone on the journey.

The election of Barack Obama as president should encourage us to have more of that "audacity to hope," that Obama's former pastor Jeremiah Wright preached about so eloquently some years ago (Obama borrowed that phrase from Wright to be the title of his book). I believe that the burden has lifted enough so that we can glance into the Promised Land and, with the audacity to hope, come to believe that something has really changed in America.

I now have the audacity to hope that children of color can dream about the future with an imagination less restricted by racism. I now have the audacity to hope that people can discover new spaces and new language for conversing on racism and reconciliation. I now have the audacity to hope that young people will choose to live in diverse communities, dismantle institutional racism, and produce policies of inclusion that lead to the erasure of racism over time so that each generation is less racist and more reconciled. And I even have the audacity to hope that more whites will welcome an African American pastor to oversee their intimate spiritual concerns because of the positive experience of a black president as their leader.

My son, a student at New York University, celebrated both his nineteenth birthday and the election of Obama in Times Square on election night; November 4, 2008. Like Obama, my son has a parent who is white and a parent who is black. The election of Obama opens the door for multiracial people in our society to embrace the fullness of their identity without renouncing the reality of racism. My son, with his big Afro hairstyle, felt some of the burden lift off of his future so that he might more often experience himself as a human being in society. With greater diversity, less racism, and more reconciliation, we will need new ways to blend our cultural realities in what the South Africa antiapartheid activists were calling "nonracialism" in the 1980s, what Latin Americans call the process of *mestizaje*, or what the Caribbean islanders refer to as "creolization." The Obama generation will find fresh ways to blend cultures, and multiracial and multicultural people will be at the forefront of this process.

In his inaugural address, President Obama proclaimed, "We cannot help but believe that the old hatreds shall someday pass; that the lines of tribe shall soon dissolve; that as our world grows smaller, our humanity shall reveal itself." He envisions a time when the burden of racism will be lifted for more than a moment and we will discover our shared humanity as we walk into a promised land of reconciliation.

His words echo the core of the gospel of Jesus Christ. The apostle Paul said that through his death and resurrection, Jesus Christ has "broken down the dividing wall...that he might create in himself one new humanity" (Ephesians 2:14–15). Jesus Christ has been in the business of lifting burdens and leading people to reconciled communities since the first century. Barack Obama is the most recent witness on a long journey.

NOTE

1. This article first appeared in a shorter version in the *Christian Century*, December 30, 2008.

15
DREAMS FROM OUR FATHERS

RAPHAEL WARNOCK

I borrow for the title of this sermon a variation on the title of a book by Barack Obama titled *Dreams from My Father*. It is a strikingly honest and beautifully written book that offers up the autobiographical reflections of a young man in search of himself amid the robust race consciousness of America. In a world conceived in stark binary terms—black or white, African or American—he was a biracial child reared by his white mother from Kansas and, at an existential level, in search of his black father from Kenya. Like all of us, he was trying to make sense of and wrest meaning from the complex strands of his own story.

But as Obama tells his own story with wisdom and insight, a complex story of race, identity, and inheritance, he also tells the story of America. In a real sense, this young author, who would later be elected president, tells the story of America and of our fathers and mothers. Our fathers and mothers—black and white, Jew and Gentile, male and female, straight and gay, slave and free. There are the Native Americans and the rest of us Americans, all of whom are immigrants, some voluntary and others involuntary.

Some came from Western Europe and the Eastern bloc. Others came from Mexico and Haiti. Some came earlier, and others have been coming lately. But we all are here together! And this is no place for parochialism, provincialism, or prejudice. This is America! Even in the wake of the election and inauguration of the nation's first African American, some people have yet to get the memo. This is America—a wonderfully complex and complicated story—and all of us are shaped in and stalked by the dreams of our fathers.

the audacity of faith

Isn't it wonderful that at long last we have sitting in the Oval Office "a dreamer in chief"? Cynicism is easy. It is particularly easy to be cynical in times like these. But it takes a tough mind and a tender heart to hold on to hope. It takes audacity to dream and to believe. It takes faith and courage and tenacity to see visions and dream dreams. Thank God we have a dreamer in chief. And thank God for Martin Luther King Jr. and others who dreamed dreams long before him. For dreams cause us to move beyond the realm of the present and reach toward possibility.

Dreams are, by their very nature, an affront to the status quo. Dreams are God's way of calling us to holy discontentment with things as they are. Dreams urge us on to righteousness and restlessness with the world as we know it. Dreams are the subtle songs of the soul that echo the vast distance between who we are and who we, by the grace of God, might become. Langston Hughes said it best:

> Hold fast to dreams, for if dreams die,
> Life is a broken-winged bird that cannot fly.
> Hold fast to dreams, for if dreams go,
> Life is a barren field, frozen with snow.

The fact is, freedom would never come to fulfillment and Barack Obama as president never would have been possible were it not for the one who dared challenge the conscience of a nation with four simple words: "I have a dream." So thank God for the dreams of Dr. King those who came before him. The prophet Joel said, "Your old men shall dream dreams" (Joel 2:28). Thank God for the dreams of our fathers and our mothers.

We should also thank God for Joseph, that blessed biblical prototype of a dreamer. You remember Joseph. From his youth God blessed him with wonderful gifts. Like our brother Martin, he was able to dream dreams and see visions. Not only did Joseph have big dreams, but he also had a "bad" coat, a wonderful mosaic of many colors. Like Martin, he saved his brothers though they had sought to destroy him. And that's how it often is with dreamers.

We tend to feel threatened by them, and so we would rather destroy them than have them destroy the status quo. That's how we deal with folks who dare to think outside of the box, to move outside of "the cave."

In Plato's allegory of the cave, the philosopher describes the process of enlightenment in this way. He says, in essence, that it is akin to a man having sat all of his life with his compatriots, chained together and with no view of reality except that of shadows from the outside world flickering against the wall of a cave. If that person were to venture outside of the cave, the process of enlightenment would be painful and difficult for him to bear. And returning to his fellows to explain what he now knows that would be difficult for them to hear. Plato argues that "if they could lay hands on the man who was trying to set them free and lead them up, they would kill him."

So it is with dreamers. So it is with those who seek to push us outside of the cave to force us to think outside of the box. That is why Joseph's brothers tried to destroy him. But in the end, he saved them and all of Egypt. Now at long last, he is at his journey's end. He has lived to be an old man with children, grandchildren, and great-grandchildren. As this dreamer speaks, he offers up inspiration and instruction about:

OUR FREEDOM

I hear him say to his brothers, "I am about to die, but God will …bring you up out of this land to the land that he swore to Abraham, to Isaac and to Jacob." These are instructive words, because Joseph has done pretty well in Egypt. He has become the prime minister and was right next to the king. But he knew that God had something bigger and badder in mind. For the moment Joseph's people are doing okay in Egypt, but ultimately they are headed to Canaan. The dreamer is teaching us that freedom is always just over the horizon. As a matter of fact, freedom is not a destination but a journey. Freedom is always beckoning us to come up higher and experience new vistas of promise and possibility.

That's the story of America. Our nation was conceived in liberty, but from the very beginning there was an ugly crack in the Liberty Bell. Someone has wondered aloud how the great patriot Patrick Henry might have responded when he said, "Give me liberty or give me death," only to hear his slave respond by saying, "Me, too!"

Freedom is a journey, and it's always just over the horizon. Whites landing on these shores thought they had arrived at it, but then black folks spoke up and said, "Wait a minute, me, too!" Self-congratulatory men thought they had it down pat until the women's suffrage movement came saying, "Wait, me, too!" We Christians were largely unconscious of our religious bigotry and the ways in which we were inhospitable to those who embrace other ways to the center, until Jews, Muslims, Hindus, and others began to say, "Wait, me, too!" Well-able folks have, with sheer stupidity, once dared to place outside their houses of worship and other public places signs that said, "Whosoever will, let them come," but with no ramps, no lifts, and no sensitivity to differently abled people. They had to rise up some years ago and say, "Wait a minute, me, too!"

Harry Emerson Fosdick, that great preacher of New York's Riverside Church, used to say, "Time makes ancient good uncouth." He's right. Yet, there is always the temptation to rest in Egypt, not recognizing that it is Egypt! Joseph says, "Keep moving! And take my bones with you!" Freedom is the looming horizon beckoning us and bidding us come a little higher.

But then hear the dreamer speak and see him as he offers up inspiration and instruction concerning:

OUR FATHERS

The Bible says that Joseph's great-grandchildren were born on his knees. Joseph died, but before he did a whole new generation was born on his knees. They were their own generation, and they would make their own path. But they belonged to him. Like them, all of us sit on the knees and stand on the shoulders of our ancestors. They gave birth to us, and we would do well to remember them in this brand-new day.

We remember black slaves who came through slavery and segregation saying, "I ain't gon' let nobody turn me round." We sit on their knees and stand on their shoulders.

Then there were the Jewish immigrants who came through the Holocaust saying, "Never again." We sit on their knees and stand on their shoulders. We sit on the knees and stand on the shoulders of our fathers and mothers!

We sit on the knees of Schwerner, Chaney, and Goodman—two Jews and an African American who died fighting for freedom in Mississippi. We also sit on the knees of Viola Liuzzo; the wife of a Detroit union worker who, like other white people, died fighting for the just cause of civil rights.

On this day when we celebrate an election victory, we cannot forget about Medgar Evers who died in his own driveway for the crime of registering black people to vote. Nor can we forget about James Meredith who marched against fear or Fannie Lou Hamer who stood up in 1968 and told the whole nation, "I'm sick and tired of being sick and tired!" We sit on their knees and stand on their shoulders.

We must thank God for Rabbi Abraham Joshua Heschel who used to talk about "spiritual grandeur and moral excellence." We remember Rabbi Heschel who, when he marched with Dr. King, said he felt as if his feet were praying! And then there is the dreamer himself, Martin Luther King Jr. who, on the night before his death, said, "I've been to the mountaintop....I've seen the Promised Land....I may not get there with you....But we as a people will get to the Promised Land."

In other words, keep moving! Keep on keeping on. And take the spirit of the struggle with you! And when we as a nation stand tall it is because we are standing on the shoulders of our fathers and our mothers!

Finally, hear the dreamer as he offers up inspiration and instruction concerning:

OUR FUTURE

Our future is tied together and our future is in the hands of God. Martin Luther King Jr. said, "We must learn to live together as brothers and sisters or we will perish separately like fools." He used to talk about the World House. He said, "One day we must come to see that peace is not merely a distant goal that we seek but a means by which we arrive at that goal." Black folk and white folk need to hear that. Palestinians and Jews, warring this very night, need to hear that! They need to hear it in Siderot and in Gaza. The dreamer said, "Peace is not merely a distant goal that we seek, but a means by which we arrive at the goal." It's difficult. We yet have a ways to go. But Joseph the dreamer says keep moving and "God will come to you" and lead you all the way!

16
CAN WE BELIEVE IN AMERICA?

LUIS CORTÉS JR.

In 1963 as a child in the third grade, I was told I could be president of the United States because it was a democracy. At home, my father did not discourage me, but he did not believe it—not because I was not smart enough but because I was his son, a Hispanic, and in America that would not do. When my daughter was told in 1987 and my son in 1991 that they could be president of this country, they believed it, but her grandfather and I, her father, did not—not because they were not smart enough but because they, like their father and grandfather, are Hispanic, and in America that would not do. Ah, but in 2011 my grandson will enter first grade and he will be told he can be president, and his father, grandfather, and great-grandfather will all smile—because for the first time in our lives we can believe it. For you see, he is Hispanic and in America that will do.

For many people, the *promise* of America has never equaled the *reality* of America. However, since the Obama election that has changed. The integration mythology is closer at hand, and the opportunity to achieve is, after all, more in our individual control than ever before in this nation's history.

In 1968 I was entering my teenage years, living in Black Harlem as one of the few Hispanics in an African American community. As a student at Frederick Douglass Junior High School I knew the world of racial strife in a personal way—in the war between minorities in poverty. It was a unique perspective to grow up with. Young African American teachers spoke to us about how change was needed in our nation and about the struggles past and present that confronted "us." As a Latino I was included in the struggle for self-awareness, self-actualization, ethnic power, and all the social theories and ideas that ruled that time. In the four decades since then, I have witnessed much that is new and much that is the same. I now live in a country in which the majority of its voters chose a man of color—a verifiable "mixed breed" to lead our nation as president.

In the America of my youth, a mixed-racial origin was always considered "black." Today there is an openness to looking at race differently. The context in which the race dialogue takes place is one that has changed through intermarriage and the sheer growth of racial and ethnic minorities in our nation. The election of Barack Obama as president of the United States may well be regarded as what Malcolm Gladwell would call the tipping point in America's long striving to reach a comfort with its racial identity.

Writing a reflection piece on the meaning of the election of Barack Obama just a few months into his presidency is fraught with danger. What I write may be outdated before this piece even gets into print. I have been asked to reflect on Barack Obama's ascendance to the mantle of leadership, to consider him as the fulfillment of Dr. Martin Luther King's dream or to compare him with Abraham Lincoln. As a Latino, I see neither of these as reality, but I rejoice in the possibilities. Allow me to explain.

The King legacy is an appropriate historical reference point from which to examine this election, although Obama's election is by no means the fulfillment of Dr. King's dream. The question is "Have we arrived in the Promised Land?" The problems of immigration have torn our country apart as we seek to extradite 15 million men, women, and children who are American citizens. Despite billions of dollars spent on education, health care, and various social issues, hundreds of economically disadvantaged neighborhoods are ruled by illiteracy, hunger, and violence. A significant number of those neighborhoods are racial-ethnic minority communities that receive fewer tax dollars for education, so their malnourished children are relegated to inferior public schools. Should these children of immigrant or impoverished families join the statistics of those who become victims of gang violence or who never learn to read beyond the sixth- or seventh-grade level, then they will never have the opportunity to be president of the United States. Inadequacies such as these are not addressed by the election of Obama as president.

Yes, this may well be the beginning of a postracial era, but the Obama election may instead be an anomaly or worse—business as usual. Millions of Americans would love to envision Obama's election as an absolution for the legacy of slavery or at least as a sign of the end of American xenophobia. But there are millions more who exist in urban and rural poverty, as well as those who may have reached economic parity but still suffer from the scourge of racial and ethnic prejudice, and these millions know better than to ascribe so much to a single election. Hispanic hate crimes, racial profiling, and crimes against immigrants have been on the rise, especially as our economy has hit hard times. American xenophobia and racial hatred for Hispanic people keeps us very far from the Promised Land.

Still, while President Obama's election has not signified the arrival of Dr. King's dream, it *is* a sign that we have taken a significant stride toward the fulfillment of what we have taught all our children. The American integration myth has begun to become a historical truism: in America, even the older generations are beginning to believe that any of their children *can* become president.

What about the persistent comparison of President Obama to Abraham Lincoln? This insistence, which has no real parallel in our history, creates many problems—for us as an American people and for Barack Obama as he embarks in his presidency. Americans need to come to grips with our cultural proclivity to equate celebrity with heroism. Our country's penchant for sensationalizing every aspect of news has led many to allude (or state outright) that President Obama is our greatest president since Lincoln—or at least to name Obama as the successor to Lincoln's legacy. I am still waiting to learn on what basis this conclusion can be reached. Comparisons to Lincoln can or should be made only *after* President Obama moves out of the Oval Office, not on the day of his inauguration.

Most Americans seem hopeful that Barack Obama will rise beyond the level of his oratorical giftedness and in fact become one of the greatest presidents in our nation's history. Certainly, the case

the audacity of faith

can be made for him being one of the greatest presidential orators, and obviously, he has made history for becoming our first black president. But, President Barack Obama has not yet saved the Union. Granted, he has been elected at a time that presents a unique opportunity to do so and to set a new course for America in this century! However, I believe it is unfair to saddle any president with the expectation of being equal to or better than the man whom many agree was the greatest of all US presidents; Abraham Lincoln.

President Obama himself has not run from that challenge, and unquestionably he is faced with sufficient challenges that offer opportunities to respond in a way that may earn him a ranking among our greatest American presidents. Great challenges are often the means to achieving greatness. A Middle Eastern war provides opportunity to put his personal stamp on American foreign policy; an economic crisis allows him to have an impact on the American capitalist system, not to mention the challenges of providing universally affordable health care, educational alternatives for economically disadvantaged children, and supporting an aging population by reconfiguring the social security system—all of which present President Obama with an opportunity to make his mark on American domestic policies. A broken and unfair immigration system gives Obama the chance to address American xenophobia, nativism, and racism. Global warming and the energy crisis will provide him an opportunity to generate an energy policy that will affect the future of the environment, not only in the US but in the world. President Obama will have to do all this while trying to create bipartisan support. He will have to attempt this without becoming more beholden to the labor unions that invested millions of dollars in his candidacy. He will endeavor to do this while we are in the midst of the greatest eco-nomic challenge we have faced since the Great Depression.

My prayer for President Obama, our nation, and our world is that in January 2017 I can say to my grandson, who will be eleven years old, "Grandson, you have lived to see the greatest president that this nation has ever had. You now have an example to follow. Work hard, Grandson…for some day you can be president."

PART III
Prophetic Rumblings for President BARACK OBAMA

17
NO DAYS OFF

EMILIE M. TOWNES

MATTHEW 25:34-40

many of us know this list
    when i was hungry you gave me food
    when i was thirsty you gave me something to drink
    when i was a stranger you welcomed me
    when i was naked you gave me clothing
    when i was sick you took care of me
just as you did it to one of the least of these who are
members of *my* family, you did it to me
now, i have always been amazed at how many times and
how many people fight to be counted among the least of these
when God's judgment is looming
    or the gains and privileges we have managed to
    accumulate
        however large or small
            are being threatened or challenged or named
    we are much like the five foolish bridesmaids and the one
slave in the parables just before this passage from matthew who are
too late and too unimaginative
    and totally missing the point of what it means at be
    inheritors of the kingdom, the realm of God
    we are called to live in righteousness, knowing that what

     the audacity of faith

we have right now is not God's final word for us
to be inheritors of God's realm means that
we *yearn* for that light in the darkness
to shine in our hearts and in the ministry of the church
our faith and our witness should not be easily checked at
the door of gerrymandered elections or specious claims of weapons
of mass destruction that are part of an evil swill
of debt in the trillions
an economic perfect storm
domestic programs like education, health care,
reproductive health, and welfare looking more like the
bopping head dolls of carnage
as refusing to have a meaningful, constructive, strategic,
and spiritually deep conversation on race and racism
so it is easy to forget the ongoing obscenity of the
aftermath of when the levees broke in new orleans
the disaster of a plan that unfolded in new orleans in
particular was a grand scale of failing to live an active
corporate witness of matthew's words to us
a white man and woman were captioned "finding" food
a black man was captioned "looting"
all three were carrying food, not t.v. sets, gameboys,
or rims
what is looting when all the governmental mechanisms
have broken down and left you to die—hungry, thirsty, alone,
naked, sick—unwelcome in your country, unwelcome in your city,
unwelcome in your neighborhood
matthew calls us to righteousness, not to performing a
minstrel show of holified bunkum
you and i are being called to be the leaders who will
change our world beginning yesterday, beginning now
and we no longer have the focus of the civil rights
movement in our hands
we no longer have buffoons like bull connor whose
behavior was so obvious that all God's children could see
he wasn't right

we no longer have the martins and malcolms and ellas and fanny lous to lead us

we are who God's got

and we have the ability to shake the foundations with our witness

we are the prophets who stand in the gap and demand of ourselves and others, to live our ideals of freedom, justice, and equality for all

to stand with the least of these who are members of the family of God

we've got issues and we have the spiritual and prophetic resources to deal with them if we lean into our faith and put our trust in the fact that God has called us here

and God never leaves us abandoned or alone in that call

there are no days off!

even when there are roadblocks of ignorance and detours of complacency put in our way

we may face stop signs that would tell us our commitment to break free of society's hatreds and fears is utopian

we may find yellow lights that tell us the work is finished now that we have elected a *nice* black man president

we may face the sharp curves of indifference, arrogance, ignorance, and empty-headedness masquerading as mission, justice, love, hope, and peace

we may get caught on the warning tracks of confused vision, confused strategies, and sometimes not having a clue

we may get behind some slow-moving vehicles on the road that continue to spawn hate crimes, think diversity is building

a weak social fabric for our country, and admitting our culpability in all manner of isms is a social statement rather than our confessional cry to God

but we never reach a dead end, for our means of transportation is the glory line

that always reaches its destination—so it is up to each of us not to get off too soon or at the wrong stop

the audacity of faith

for we are being shaped and molded by a spectacular savior
who offers us life over death
and witness over complacency
and the strength, weakness, wisdom, and foolishness to
stare at the prejudices and racisms we have stuffed *way* down in us
and begin to look inward and outward and work with
each other
while being held in God's spanless hands
and step into the lives of the least of these who are found
in the many-colored spectrum of our humanity

there are no days off!
now i believe that most of us
are hankering for a faith that comes from seeking to live in
righteousness
to move beyond a ritualized, sterilized, codified, and
cul-de-sac faith
to one that comes from the heart and soul
this faith is so dynamic, strong, so tough that we can craft
a community of witnesses from it
made up of peoples of all racial ethnic groups
both genders and intersex
varied lifestyles and abilities
different political and theological agendas
from all levels of the class structure
documented and undocumented
all ages
and on and on into the richness of our living
a community of righteousness striving to reach out to the
least of these
witnessing through our spirituality and our sense of justice
demanding the best of who we can be as a church
refusing to accept maudlin loathing as divine
commandments
when folks are hungry, thirsty, outcast, naked, sick
when we turn remembering king's legacy into a one-day-

a-year feel-good time-paid-holiday celebration of inept kumbayas and sashaying alleluias

when we believe that one election in which we finally did the right thing has solved all of our issues

no, no, no, my brothers and sisters, the fact of the matter is we are our issues, and wherever we go, there they are

we cannot set up one very human man, president obama, to be our stand-in for atonement or our bulwark of salvation

we are the work we must do in digging deep within our hearts and souls to find the people God is calling us to be

and once we find those people, live our lives as torchlights of mercy, lanterns of hope, beacons of love, and embers of justice

there are no days off, my brothers and sisters!

stepping into faithful righteousness is ever renewing,

for in doing so we live and witness out of God's grace-filled forgiveness

and even in the midst of our utter humanity we can reach out to the poor

the dispossessed

the lonely

the rejected

as brothers and sisters and not as a mission project

for we realize they are us and *each* of us is called by God to be all of who we can be and beyond what we are

and we must never forget that our faith is to be lived from the inside out

to be lived from our center, our soul, our hearts

and that means that if we err in our witness, it is to be on the side of trying to reach beyond what we thought possible

and not because we settled for less than what we are capable of

living in faithful righteousness holds us together

it gives us the pith of our community

it sustains us through God's relentless love

there are no days off!

the audacity of faith

no matter the depth of our great hope that we have
changed as a nation
there are no days off
we must step into the great challenges we have before us
there are no days off
we must live in the promises and refuse to accept a trail of
broken promises as signs of salvation
there are no days off
we can destroy hunger
we can conquer hate
there are no days off
we are the righteous standing with the least of these
there are no days off
no matter what they say about whether you are married,
divorced, single, straight, gay, lesbian, or who knows what
there are no days off
no matter what they say about how well you dress and
how well-behaved your spouse and children are
there are no days off
no matter what they say about your voice being too high
a pitch or too low a pitch
there are no days off
no matter where you come from in life and where you
hope to go in this life and beyond
there are no days off
no matter what color you are
there are no days off
no matter where your people come from
there are no days off
no matter how many times you are called too tender-
hearted or too concerned about "those people"
there are no days off
no matter how many times politicians and public figures
and other alleged christians pick up the bible to abuse it and then
use it to ratify their personal wickedness
there are no days off

no matter what the world hands us, we give back love
we stand for goodness
we live our faith
we live with integrity
we live God's grace large
we stand with the least of these
we build bridges of salvation that can carry the depth and
breadth of humanity over them
there are no days off
for "the future started yesterday, and we're already late"
(John Legend)
ummph...ummph...ummph

amen.

18

PREACHER-PROPHET OBAMA

WILLIAM H. WILLIMON

"Do you really think that a sermon changes anything? Isn't preaching irrelevant in the modern world?" That's what a preacher asked during my workshop for preachers in Massachusetts last fall. I responded, "We are preparing to elect a man president of our country who is very young, who has held no important positions, except for a short run as a senator from a questionable state, all on the basis of 'he talks real good.' Don't tell me that nobody cares about preaching!"

We are rather pitiful in our adulation of our new president's ability to use the English language. Our praise for Obama's eloquence is related to our former president's great difficulty putting together a sentence. Still, as someone who talks for a living, a brother to Jeremiah Wright, I would like to say a word for the power of the word as exemplified in Obama.

How ironic that a major issue during the campaign was Obama's pastor. Obama defenders said the ruckus over some of Jeremiah Wright's sermons was a distraction from more important issues. Obama's detractors found Wright's sermons to be deeply frightening.

I happen to believe that Wright's detractors, in ways they are too ignorant to know, were right. Fox News does not understand that Wright speaks from within a grand prophetic tradition in which the powerful are mocked and the powerless are given a means to grieve their present situation and to celebrate what a just God can do. The Hebrew prophets attempted to move the world, tear down empires, and lift up the oppressed on the basis of nothing but words. Biblical prophets were not carping social critics; they were poets who believed that the Word of God can create new worlds. They believed the story of creation as told in Genesis was true: God creates something out of nothing, a world out of chaos just through words: "Let there be light."

When Obama stood before the United States Capitol on January 20, 2009, he also stood within that prophetic-poetic tradition. A prophet brings new worlds to speech, takes us to a place we would not have gone on our own, all on the basis of nothing but words: "Words have been spoken during rising tides of prosperity and the still waters of peace...amidst gathering clouds and raging storms."[1]

Like the eighth-century B.C. Hebrew prophets, after an opening encomium on America, Obama spoke words of judgment, criticizing not only those in power but also us much-discussed "ordinary Americans" who had been the focus of much of the rhetoric of his opponents in the fall campaign: "Our economy is badly weakened, a consequence of greed and irresponsibility on the part of some, but also our collective failure to make hard choices and prepare the nation for a new age....Our health care is too costly; our schools fail too many; and each day brings further evidence that the ways we use energy strengthen our adversaries and threaten our planet."[2]

I was surprised by the new president's candor: "Less measurable but no less profound is a sapping of confidence across our land— a nagging fear that America's decline is inevitable, and that the next generation must lower its sights. Today I say to you that the challenges we face are real. They are serious and they are many. They will not be met easily or in a short span of time."[3]

People in power tend to put a happy face on everything—we have never had it so good. Administration press releases tell us that we live in the best of all possible worlds, brought to us by the beneficence of the present administration. Those on top tend toward optimistic assessments of the present moment. They can afford to be happy; after all, they are in power.

Prophets like Amos or Jeremiah on the other hand teach people that it's okay to cry. They publicly process grief. (This is the big prophetic move that Fox News never got about Jeremiah Wright. I also note that many Republican spokespersons are criticizing Obama for his "pessimism.") Grief is not the prophets' goal, but rather an essential, unavoidable step toward dreaming and new vision. We cannot envision the possibility of a new, better world if we are unable to let go of the old world. And that relinquishment will probably entail some tears.

From judgment the prophetic preacher moves to a new vision. The vision does not lie about our present situation, but it casts a prophetic preview of the world that shall, by God's grace, come upon us. This is not facile optimism: it is a courageous determination to rise above the present moment. The prophet dares to dream:

> On this day, we gather because we have chosen hope over fear, unity of purpose over conflict and discord....We remain a young nation, but in the words of Scripture, the time has come to set aside childish things. The time has come to reaffirm our enduring spirit; to choose our better history; to carry forward that precious gift, that noble idea, passed on from generation to generation: the God-given promise that all are equal, all are free, and all deserve a chance to pursue their full measure of happiness.
>
> In reaffirming the greatness of our nation, we understand that greatness is never a given. It must be earned....It has been the risk-takers, the doers, the makers of things— some celebrated but more often men and women obscure in their labor—who have carried us up the long, rugged path towards prosperity and freedom.
>
> We will build the roads and bridges, the electric grids and digital lines that feed our commerce and bind us together. We will restore science to its rightful place, and wield technology's wonders to raise health care's quality and lower its cost. We will harness the sun and the winds and the soil....And we will transform our schools and colleges and universities....All this we can do. And all this we will do.

Now, there are some who question the scale of our ambitions—who suggest that our system cannot tolerate too many big plans. Their memories are short. For they have forgotten what this country has already done.[4]

Note that the preacher-prophet casts a new vision on the basis of historical remembrance. The prophets of Israel were not progressive social liberals; they were, in their own way, traditionalists. "Remember," "recall," "return," are favorite prophetic imperatives. The prophets do not call for something new that leaves behind the old; rather, they call for a restoration of the best of the tradition, for a return to the vision that gave birth to a chosen people. Obama clearly stands in this tradition. While American history is replete with instances of how that "chosen people" metaphor made mischief, Obama works it to assert that we are the "almost chosen people": We have been given gifts, but we have not always been true to those gifts. Nevertheless, we can be.

In cadences that sound almost biblical, the speech now picks up energy and rhythm in remembrance:

> For us, they packed up their few worldly possessions and traveled across oceans in search of a new life.
> For us, they toiled in sweatshops and settled the West; endured the lash of the whip and plowed the hard earth.
> For us, they fought and died, in places like Concord and Gettysburg.[5]

Then Obama mentions our religious diversity as one of our national strengths:

> We are a nation of Christians and Muslims, Jews and Hindus—and non-believers. We are shaped by every language and culture, drawn from every end of this earth; and because we have tasted the bitter swill of civil war and segregation, and emerged from that dark chapter stronger and more united, we cannot help but believe that the old

hatreds shall someday pass; that the lines of tribe shall soon dissolve; that as the world grows smaller, our common humanity shall reveal itself; and that America must play its role in ushering in a new era of peace.[6]

What bothers me about this section is that it suggests a return to American exceptionalism—we are a very special nation, and therefore we have a responsibility to share American righteousness all over the world, whether the world wants it or not. Even as I write this, our new president has ordered a massive surge in the troops in Afghanistan, determined to bring that unruly nation in line with our righteous national purposes.

The prophets of Israel not only brought new worlds to speech, they also taught a nation to grieve and to dream. The prophets reminded a nation that it lived under the sovereign judgments of God. That was a key prophetic element lacking in President Obama's speech. He characterized national resolve in this way: "This is the source of our confidence—the knowledge that God calls on us to shape an uncertain destiny."[7]

Of course, a national political leader cannot call upon God for any real help in survival of the nation, because we are a nation that has permitted religion to be free only if faith is reduced to something personal and private. Faith in public, faith in a God who actually does something, is no longer permissible. Therefore, the best we can hope for, when God appears in a speech of this sort, is the deistic God of our so-called Founding Fathers, the God who is gracious, who has benevolently bestowed upon us some originating good gifts, but who has no strong opinions about the way we conduct ourselves.

Since there is no longer a God who judges or intrudes, all this God can do is to call "on us to shape an uncertain destiny." It's up to us to be God now.

With hope and virtue, let us brave once more the icy currents, and endure what storms may come. Let it be said by our children's children that when we were tested we refused to let this journey end, that we did not turn back nor did we falter; and with eyes fixed on the horizon and God's grace upon us, we carried forth that great gift of freedom and delivered it safely to future generations.[8]

Though much criticized, I liked the rather somber, restrained tone of Obama's speech. But I was troubled by the rather conventional upbeat American call to arms and optimistic swagger of America as hope for the world.

Of course, like President Obama; I'm a Christian, and like him, I believe that Jesus Christ is the hope for the world. Like President Obama, I have difficulty saying that in public gatherings where most of those present think that their personal judgments are sovereign and their actions in the world are the only action.

Still, I wish that our new president had ventured the full prophetic plunge into the countercultural prophetic truth that God, not nations, rules the world and that all of us, even at our best, stand under the judgments of a righteous God whose ways are higher than our ways.

NOTES

1. Barack Obama, "Inaugural Address," Washington, DC, January 20, 2009. http://www.nytimes.com/2009/01/20/us/politics/20text-obama.html (accessed March 17, 2009).

2. Ibid.

3. Ibid.

4. Ibid.

5. Ibid.

6. Ibid.

7. Ibid.

8. Ibid.

19

A HOPE THAT DOES NOT DISAPPOINT:
An Obama Presidency and Romans 5:5

WILLIAM H. MYERS

And hope does not disappoint us. —Romans 5:5 NIV

Not since the election of John Fitzgerald Kennedy has an electorate been so energized and inspired to hope again. That is the first thing to be considered as we witness the election of Barack Hussein Obama. One cannot escape the obvious or the subtle historical similarities. A young, highly intelligent, charismatic, inspiring Irish Catholic liberal from the Northeast thinking he could be president. A young, highly intelligent, charismatic, inspiring African American liberal from Chicago politics thinking he could be president. Given these similarities we can't help but ask, what will be the end of the hope inspired this time around? What is the basis of it; what is its foundation; what are its goals; will it be a hope that does not disappoint?

We heard much about hope during the campaign, but very soon after the election, the word *expectations* started to dominate. "Lowering of expectations" became the watchword. The management of expectations is an attempt to cap hope, but it is a slippery slope, and the collapsing of Christian hope into political hope is even more dangerous. We must seek to expose these realities or, better, to "rip the veil off the veiling," to use a very elastic metaphor as utilized overtly or subtly by W. E. B. DuBois (*The Souls of Black Folk*), Toni Morrison (*Beloved*), and Vincent Wimbush ("We Shall Make Our Own Future Texts," in *True to Our Native Land*).

Perhaps there is no better character to utilize as a heuristic device to juxtapose these two historic moments and to rip the veil and expose the dangers than Martin Luther King Jr. King was very adept at pointing out the dangers that occur following the elation of raised expectations turning into disappointment and despair from the failure to bring them to life.

He observed how after the elation of Kennedy's election in 1960 both parties marked time in the cause of justice. As to that newly elected president in whom so much hope was placed, King said that if he didn't back down, he certainly backed away from key campaign promises.[1]

In yet another historic moment, what President Lyndon Johnson called one of the greatest historic events in the nation's history—the 1965 Voting Rights Act—King observed the following:

> One year later they [black protesters] were being stoned in a Chicago suburb. Negro leaders involved in the resistance had lost their jobs, the political backlash was that the other party elected political clowns full of bigotry to key political offices. The expectation of swift justice for murdered civil rights workers in the South turned into swift acquittals. Northern and western youth turned to violence in their cities, and *Ramparts* magazine concluded that after ten years of civil rights movement, Negroes were no better off.[2]

King reminds us to stay awake during a revolution lest we miss not only the revolution but essential, critical insights about the moment. Speaking about the Vietnam War, King said:

> I am convinced that it is one of the most unjust wars that has ever been fought in the history of the world. Our involvement in the war in Vietnam has torn up the Geneva Accord....It has played havoc with our domestic destinies. This day we are spending five hundred thousand dollars to kill every Vietcong soldier...while we spend only fifty-three dollars a year for every person characterized as

the audacity of faith

poverty-stricken….And here we are ten thousand miles away from fighting for the so-called freedom of the Vietnamese people when we have not even put our own house in order….Something must be done quickly….We have alienated ourselves from other nations so we end up morally and politically isolated in the world.[3]

Is King still alive; did he just pen these words the other day? If we were to change some names, it would be as if he were speaking of current events. History is trying to speak to us. The day after the election a financial commentator opined that Obama was not being elected commander in chief or president, but more of a trustee in chief of a bankrupt nation. This has led me to ponder what disappointments will inevitably follow a campaign full of promises and hope.

In contrast to King's one-year-later litany of disappointments, our chant is one week later: economic catastrophe, escalations of wars, politics as usual in the face of attempted change, greed as usual in the midst of disaster, the backing down or backing away from campaign promises, trillions spent on wars and Wall Street while pennies are spent on Main Street and the poor. Obama said, "I won"; Republicans said, "We don't care." Wall Street CEOs and bankers said, "Give us the people's money, and we will do what we want." Appointees said, "We don't need to follow the rules." And the millions of people without jobs and with homes in foreclosure said, "Where is the help? Where is the hope?" Is this the recipe for a hope that disappoints?

In a critical passage in the letter to the Romans (chapter 5), Paul gives us the only foundation for a hope that does not disappoint (literally, "put to shame"). A Judeo-Christian perspective argues that only a faith centered in God—and for Christians, in the resurrected Jesus of Nazareth—does not disappoint. This hope is a certain hope, not the uncertain hope and expectations of political realities. With political hope someone will always be disappointed.

What this hope is based on is stated in verses 3-5. This is not an abstract hope, but one grounded in the knowledge of the Christian experience, grounded in the hope of the glory of God. It is a hope that allows one to endure afflictions. These afflictions are not ones that destroy the person, but instead they build up the endurance and perseverance that allow them to emerge with tested character. This hope is so certain that Paul, this apostle who argues against boasting earlier in this letter (see 1 Corinthians 1–3), argues that the Christian can boast of its certainty. The foundation for this boast, however, is in the blessed grace and certain love of God. This truly is a hope that will not put one to shame.

This is not abstract futuristic eschatology for Paul. It is present and personal. It is present in the "now–not yet" experience of Christian faith that endures through suffering. It is personal not merely in the utilitarian individualism of Western thought, but in the agonizingly painful concern for a people, as seen in Paul's pouring out of grief for the Jewish people in Romans 9–11. There Paul himself comes to the most mystifying declaration of hope in all of his writings about the question of what God will do about the plight of his people: God will deliver every last one of them.

A large part of this nation—African Americans in particular and young people in larger numbers than ever before—cast not only their vote, but their hopes on an Obama presidency. So, too, in spirit and in heart did many from around the world, with the hope of not being disappointed as they had been for the last eight years. Can he deliver?

In less than a month, we have seen people feeling disappointed on numerous issues. We have seen many groups and individuals express disappointment in one way or another. How did all these people get disappointed so fast—women, conservatives, liberals, blacks, whites, homosexuals, heterosexuals, Republicans, Democrats, Blue Dogs, you name them?

Is it too early and too unfair to ask the question? Is this what Jeremiah Wright was trying to tell us ("he [Obama] is a politician")? Did we not want to have that conversation for fear that it would ruin "their" chance to finally get one of "their own" in the White House? What did we miss by this selective refusal to engage in a certain discourse, and what are the implications of this refusal to rip the veil of the veiling should it continue now that "our man" is in the White House?

What do these things say about Obama—reaching out to Republicans; selecting and supporting appointees who had not paid their taxes; compromising on economic bills; closing down Guantanamo, riding the fence about Geneva Accord violations in the past administration; being initially quiet on the Arab-Israeli conflict, escalating the war in Afghanistan? Is this change or just more of the same?

Barack Obama, the consummate politician (you don't get elected president of the United States and survive Chicago politics unless you are a politician—whether that ends up being good or bad, only time will tell), naively or knowingly ran into the reality of Washington politics. Politics in general and Washington politics in particular seem to soil a person. Many people who went to Washington to change it found themselves changed by it instead. Presidents are not exempt. The real question is how will the electorate and religious leaders fair this time?

Can Obama deliver on the kind of hope laid out by Paul to the Roman church and Christian faith? The obvious answer is no. Barack Obama is a politician facing some foreign and domestic political realities, the likes of which this nation has not seen in a very long time and maybe has never seen before. I have no idea whether he or this nation is ready for the afflictions that are already at hand, but we have weathered numerous other afflictions in the past.

I do know that President Obama and this nation will need much prayer. However, we must do more than merely follow the Christian mandate to pray for our political leaders. As King pushed Kennedy and Johnson, so too must African American religious leaders and all the people of God continuously press Obama to put aside political considerations and rise to a level of moral commitment and resistance, whether this be the ending of the war and withdrawal from Iraq and Afghanistan, the challenging of hegemonic greed and unbridled utilitarian individualism in America, the forceful addressing of racially motivated police brutality, or the righting of the wrong of holding people unjustly at Guantanamo.

Issues of justice do not solely rest on the shoulders of the people of God. The people of God must serve as a conscience to the nation, remembering that God calls nations, kings, and presidents to judgment as well. The people of God must press the leaders of the nation to act justly, love mercy, and walk humbly before God. Doing that will not put to shame or disappoint.

Then King's words directed at two other historic moments (1863, 1963) in our nation's history may speak yet again to another historic moment:

> Simple logic made it painfully clear that if this centennial were to be meaningful, it must be observed not as a celebration, but rather as a commemoration of the one moment in the country's history when a bold, brave *start* had been made, and a rededication to the obvious fact that urgent business was at hand—the resumption of that noble journey toward the goals reflected in the Preamble of the Constitution, the Constitution itself, the Bill of Rights and the Thirteenth, Fourteenth and Fifteenth Amendments.[4]

NOTES

1. Martin Luther King Jr., *Why We Can't Wait* (New York: Signet Classics, 1964), 20.

2 Martin Luther King Jr., *Where Do We Go from Here: Chaos or Community?* (Boston: Beacon Press, 1968), 2.

3. Martin Luther King Jr., "Remaining Awake through a Great Revolution," in *A Testament of Hope*, James M. Washington, ed., (San Francisco: HarperOne, 1990), 275–76.

4. King, *Why We Can't Wait*, 25.

20
HOPE HAS ITS REASONS

TONY CAMPOLO

Over the years, the African American community has been victimized by the oppressive treatment it has received at the hands of dominant white America, but Barack Obama does not act like a victim. Instead, he radiates the self-confidence and dignity of a man who asks no concessions for himself from those who have often held back other African Americans.

Obama's classic Philadelphia speech on racism brilliantly exemplified that he fully understood the hurts and angers of his fellow African American citizens and that his election would not mean that racism has become passé in our country. On the other hand, however, he communicated that the hope for the future lies in confession by the white establishment and forgiveness from the African American community. Our new president has asked his black brothers and sisters to leave behind the justifiable accusatory rhetoric and attitudes that may have already accomplished their purposes.

Rather than dwelling on the past, Obama calls upon all Americans to press toward the realization of the dream so well articulated by Martin Luther King. He reminds us that it was King's belief that "Black and White Together" could actualize the vision of America becoming one people with liberty and justice for all.

Recognizing that King's dream requires more than an end to social policies that have left a host of his fellow Americans outside the household of equal opportunities looking in, Barack Obama clearly goes on to indicate that ending racism requires spiritual transformations that reach into the deepest recesses of our hearts and minds. Alluding to repressed prejudices, Obama holds up his own white grandmother, who loved him dearly but still had within her (as within the most gracious among us) racist elements that had not been rooted out. Acknowledging that America has not yet met the challenge of Martin Luther King to overcome racism, Barack Obama, nevertheless, invites a new generation of Americans to live out King's ideals by dealing with these repressed prejudices with the help of God.

While President Obama may herald a new era of race relations, there are limitations as to what can be accomplished through political leadership alone. Regardless of the new visions and dreams that he inspires with his charisma, Barack Obama seems to know we will never transcend racist categorizations until there is a movement of God's Spirit among us. He echoes the prophetic imagination of Howard Thurman, one-time chaplain of Howard University, understanding that until we are transformed so as to find in one another the image of God waiting to be embraced, reconciliation between the races cannot happen.

In addition to heralding a possible new era in race relations, Barack Obama also generates hope for the fulfillment of King's dreams—that America once again would take its place as "the city on the hill," whose moral character would warrant the respect of the world. There is no question as to the expectation of most Americans that Barack Obama certainly will change our image in the eyes of people of other countries. This is something we elected him to do.

Following 9/11, America had the sympathy and goodwill of most of the nations of the world. But all of that goodwill was squandered over the next seven years as our nation embarked on a path that disregarded world opinion and behaved in ways that most of the world considered reckless. The invasion of Iraq, the ways in which that war was conducted, the lack of parity in dealing with the Palestinian-Israeli crisis, the treatment of prisoners at Guantanamo, and the rendition policies that made America a partner in the torture of terrorist suspects all led to the loss of our once high moral standing on the world scene. Now as Barack Obama takes office, there is hope that the negative images of America engendered by such actions might be overcome.

All over Africa there was dancing and cheering on November 5, 2008. In the days since, there has been a growing belief around the globe that America is about to be born again.

It remains to be seen whether or not our new president can challenge the entrenched bureaucracies of the CIA, the State Department, and the military, as he tries to usher in a new beginning for who we are and what we want to be as a nation. Yet hope for a new day in American diplomacy has spread throughout the world, from faraway Arab nations to nearby Cuba.

Barack Obama has been nurtured on Christian values ever since making a personal commitment to become a follower of Christ, but it remains to be seen how those values will mold his policies as he engages world leaders and declares how America will act in the future. The Bible says that it is righteousness that exalts a nation, and all of us as Christians should be praying that righteousness will guide our nation's policies and actions in foreign affairs under the direction of our new president.

In spite of all the optimism that accompanies our new president, there are still apprehensions and concerns that trouble some of us. First of all, Barack Obama has proposed to govern according to a philosophy of pragmatism. If by this the president means that he will be seeking ways to get things done in the most efficiently successful manner, many will applaud that philosophy.

However, I personally hope and pray that his pragmatic measures will always be critiqued by biblical principles so that God's justice will trump pragmatic efficiency when the two are in conflict. Regrettably, there are signs that this may not be the case. Barack Obama *did* go back on his word about campaign financing. He promised that his campaign would be funded with federal dollars instead of by donations from special interest groups. Even though going back on his word did enable him to raise enough money to conduct one of the most effective campaigns in American political history, that pragmatic act was a bad sign for many of us.

Consider also President Obama's adamant commitment to end the war in Iraq posthaste, which seemed to diminish somewhat as his campaign progressed. His endeavor to become more acceptable to the American electorate by becoming more politically centrist undoubtedly was the result of pragmatic necessity, but that change made a lot of us very nervous. There is increasing skepticism that the president's promise of a quick exit from Iraq is a promise that will not be kept, even though it was a primary reason many of us voted for him. There are growing signs that there will be an ongoing military presence in Iraq for the foreseeable future. For those of us who are antimilitaristic for religious reasons, this would be a great disappointment.

The economic crisis that awaited Barack Obama following his inauguration has led him also, for pragmatic reasons, to temper his commitments on behalf of the poor. Given the bailouts and loans to the banks and to the auto industries, his plans for a quick fix for our broken health care system and our inadequate schools surely will be put on the back burner. Promised increased funding for faith-based programs are likely to be shoved aside for the same reasons. To pragmatists, all such actions seem to be an absolute necessity, but to the poor, these decisions are disappointing and may lead to a disillusioning sense that Barack Obama does not keep his promises. On behalf of the poor and oppressed of America, let us pray that the needs of the poor are not neglected in the face of a fiscal crisis.

On other matters, there are some who wish that Barack Obama would be *more* pragmatic. For one, George McGovern, a former candidate for the presidency and a one-time standard bearer for the Democratic Party, told me that he hopes that the new president will exercise some pragmatic realism when it comes to the war in Afghanistan. Senator McGovern pointed out that no foreign power has been able to win a military victory in Afghanistan over the last 2,500 years. In the nineteenth and twentieth centuries, neither the British nor the Soviet Union, even at the height of their respective military prowess, were able to bring Afghanistan into submission. "It is arrogant," said Senator McGovern, "to think that we can do better." Instead, the senator proposed that America should work to contain al-Qaida rather than to kill off its members. He is of the opinion that we cannot get rid of terrorism by killing terrorists any more than it is possible to get rid of malaria by killing mosquitoes. The way to get rid of malaria is by destroying the swamps in which mosquitoes breed. So it is that the way to get rid of terrorism is to get rid of the "swamps" in which terrorists are bred—poverty, oppression, and humiliation constitute the conditions that must be stamped out if terrorism is to be eradicated from the earth.

The church has a crucial role to play as our new president takes office. Christian leaders are going to have to learn to speak truth to power without themselves becoming power brokers. Both the religious left and the religious right in the past have gone to the Oval Office conveying the impression that each had constituencies that would lend support to those in positions of power, if only their respective proposed agendas would be enacted.

Recently the religious right has played the power games more effectively. From successful efforts to bar the use of condoms as part of our country's program to fight AIDS in Africa, to making sure that pro-life judges were appointed to the seats of federal courts, the religious right has done well in achieving its goals.

The prophetic church that would best serve Barack Obama is a church that, rather than threatening to coerce with voting power, would use noncoercive means as it declares biblical truth with authority and as it calls those in power to consider what is right in the eyes of God on the simple basis *that it is right*!

There is little question that the Bible requires the leaders of nations to care for the poor. More than 2,000 Scripture verses call for justice for the poor and oppressed (see Matthew 25:31-46). In today's world, this means not only that the church must engage in acts of charity to alleviate suffering wherever it is confronted, but it must also call for changes in the macro-structures of society that often create poverty. Church leaders must call upon our new president to cancel third world debts so that the poor nations of the world can use their tax dollars to meet the needs of their indigenous people, rather than paying interest on ill-advised loans often made by dictators who have long since passed from the scene. Our new president should also be called upon to restructure trade relations so that poor nations are not left at severe disadvantage in the midst of our present global economy.

What is right may not always be popular with the electorate, and the church will not always be able to promise Barack Obama voter support if he does what the Lord requires of him. Especially during these times of an economic meltdown, what is right might run counter to our nation's economic self-interests. But the church should proclaim to Barack Obama what biblical justice requires of him, even if its voice is not heeded. Our new president should be constantly reminded by the church that, in the end, the only applause he should seek is that which comes from nail-pierced hands.

For all the condemnation of Jeremiah Wright for his ugly remarks about America, we should remember still that over his years of pastoring and preaching in the church Barack Obama called home, Rev. Dr. Wright made our new president aware of what prophetic preaching is all about. We ought not to discount Jeremiah Wright's years of biblical declarations as to what constitutes social justice because of his few sad and shocking mistakes that were brought to light during Barack Obama's campaign. Our new president needs voices like that of Dr. Wright's which will speak to him as he makes decisions that will determine America's future. President Obama needs prophets who will say with biblical authority, "Thus saith the Lord." If all the church has to offer are clergy persons who flatter Barack Obama and fail to critique his policies from scripturally prescribed perspectives, it will have failed to be the church that it ought to be.

The next few years will not only be a challenge for Barack Obama to be the kind of leader God would have him be; they will be a challenge also to the church and whether or not God's people can be who the Lord calls us to be.

21
THE HOPE THAT THE PRESENT
HAS BROUGHT US

JAMES HENRY HARRIS

I knew that Barack Obama had reached iconic status in African American culture in general, and in our house particularly, when my wife placed a framed picture of him on the mantel over the fireplace in the family room. He now occupies a place that during my childhood and youth was reserved only for Martin Luther King Jr. and Jesus Christ. I had another experience of change while watching the recent Academy Awards ceremony where persons from India and Japan were recognized for their achievements in film. On Oscar night, I began to cry as I listened to the Best Original Music Score by the dark-skinned Indian songwriter A. R. Rahman who won an Oscar for his song "Jai Ho." These two examples of my personal experience are meaningful and critically important in understanding how far the world has come (during my lifetime) in accepting people of color and not just the privileged Europeans and white Americans.

Don't get me wrong. I am skeptical about attributing any false accretions in race relations and "postracial" realities to the election of a president who identifies himself as African American although his mother is white American and his father African. During nearly three hundred years of American chattel slavery, the child was classified as the same race of his or her mother to assure that mulattoes would still be black slaves in spite of their resemblance to their fathers—the white slave masters. This system of racism and economic greed was inhuman and violently oppressive. And yet the "one-drop rule" of American jurisprudence and social custom forbade miscegenation and integration, effectively extending American slavery to the twentieth century by the establishment and practices of Jim Crow laws throughout the South.

The election of President Obama may eventually be accretive relative to race relations in America, but the immediate effects are not discernible. The unemployment rate for blacks is still disproportionate to whites, and the number of people considered homeless seems to be growing. For example, at our church in Richmond, Virginia, we serve as an intake site for those who are homeless as a part of a ministry called Congregations Around Richmond to Assure Shelter (CARITAS). We have been doing this now for fifteen years, and it appears to me that the numbers are increasing rather than decreasing on any given day. As I drive up to the church, persons are huddled under the canopy leading to the front doors of the entrance. They are male and female, black and white, old and young. Some are smoking cigarettes, others are shaking and coughing as they stand or sit in the doorway. One of our faithful servants, Sister Lenora Hicks, and the missionary leaders, alongside youth, choir members, ushers, and others, are busy preparing snacks as the homeless await the time they can enter the building to relax, eat, and fellowship before boarding a bus to be transported across town to another church that will house them until morning. This goes on seven days a week, rain or shine, from October through March throughout the city.

As I scurry into my office to escape the throngs of those gathered and to reflect on the value of this ministry, I cannot stop agonizing over the reality that stares me in the face every single day—the black poor, the homeless, the sick, the needy, the uninsured, the mentally challenged, and the hungry. Over the years, this reality has caused me a lot of anguish such that I no longer have the strength to face the oppressed without succumbing to an overwhelming sense of sadness that has almost morphed into hopelessness.

There are those in the church who wonder why I don't spend more time mingling with those who have come to get a bowl of soup and a sandwich or a hot turkey and dressing dinner at

Thanksgiving time or a snack in the evening as the homeless wait for a place to sleep at night. Well, after more than thirty years of fighting, advocating, protesting, marching, and speaking for the underprivileged, the undereducated, the underfed, the underemployed—the oppressed—I have abandoned my youthful idealism for the reality that stares me in the face every day.

Maybe the election of Barack Obama to the U.S. presidency means that I can hope again—that I will have the audacity to hope in the presence of a pandemic and engulfing nihilism that is beginning to beset even me, the preacher. These days the words of Hebrew Scripture ring incessantly in my ears: "Vanity of vanities, says the Teacher, vanity of vanities! All is vanity" (Ecclesiastes 1:2). In watching the election of Barack Obama, I could not help but think about our history as lived experience—the story of the African American in the United States. As a student of the writings of H. Richard Niebuhr and Paul Ricoeur,[1] I had to ask myself what Obama's election means in relationship to faith and history—that is, slavery, the American use of the word *nigger/nigga*, and recent events like Hurricane Katrina and the devastation of an iconic American city—New Orleans. President Obama had a lot to say about the effects of the hurricane in his book *The Audacity of Hope*.[2]

The color of suffering in America is still overwhelmingly black, and Hurricane Katrina was its most recent and obvious representation. The hurricane's effects were seen in the pain and suffering on the faces of black folks who were dazed, some frazzled and frayed by the wind and the water and by the knowledge that hopelessness and despair had engulfed them in the vortex of the swirling winds and crumbling levies. The old, the young, the poor, and the sick were mainly black. They were like slaves, bound by the chains of bureaucratic indifference from FEMA to the White House. With all the water rising and people floating and drowning, I kept thinking of the transatlantic "middle passage," because New Orleans looked like the sea—the Atlantic Ocean carrying cargoes of blacks to the point of no return.

That storm caused a lot of pain in my soul and stirred my imagination about injustice in the free world. The city was a river. The land where blacks lived looked like the Mississippi River. Those without transportation or money to escape to high ground were mainly black. There was no freedom there. At that very moment, I thought of Mark Twain's American classic *Adventures of Huckleberry Finn* and how Twain had used the word "nigger" over 220 times. I knew how Huck and Miss Watson's nigger Jim must have felt—especially Jim who felt betrayed and bamboozled by Huck. He was unequal. The hurricane got me to thinking about all kinds of atrocities and troubles. Nietzsche's fundamental insight became mine: "There is no pre-established harmony between the furtherance of truth and the well-being of mankind."[3] The truth about the levees was already well known. The elevation of the city was known, and the strength and power of Katrina were predictable.

Imagine my metaxological state of existence. I was still caught in the middle of the past and the future. I was suspended in purgatory while the folks caught in the eye of the storm were experiencing the depth of Dante's hell. It was a Sunday morning when I should have been getting ready for church, but I was in a rut, stuck in a place of powerlessness and pain. So I grabbed my pen and paper and began to write about people, places, and things that conquered my spirit. I remembered the ravages of segregation. Segregation in and of itself may not have been a bad thing, except segregation is about human nature and the oppressive acts of colonization. It was driven by the inability to acknowledge or recognize the personhood of the Other.

It was the hurricane coupled with my reading of *Adventures of Huckleberry Finn* that caused me to think so much about race and what it was like for me and so many other black folks in the South. The mind of the South was a terrible thing to run up against. But it was more than that, because past and present were being married at the altar of ambivalence, where there was no real redemption and very little hope. I could feel the rumblings in my spirit as I began again to write down my feelings in story form.[4] My imagination was on fire and my heart was sad. Reading *Adventures of Huckleberry Finn* had stirred up something I

the audacity of faith

thought was latent and under control. I thought I had successfully sublimated my seeping anger and distanced myself from the forbidden word. Surely no one had called me a nigger since long before I went to college.

Yet every time Mark Twain's characters used the word *nigger* to refer to Jim, I felt that I too was being called nigger. I was nigger Jim. I was the nigger professor. A whole heap of history was piling up on me. My knees were buckling under the weight of a word that was like an albatross around my neck. It was a harness, a steel collar, a cotton gin fan, a heavy choking weight. And when I couldn't stand it any longer, "I lit out," not in the way of Huck Finn, but in the spirit of Huck; I found freedom, not in "old rags," but in my own imagination. This is the place where freedom first begins, you know.

Not just freedom, but faith and love and hope are also domiciled in the imagination. The power of the imagination brought down the structures of slavery and enabled Abraham Lincoln to sign the Emancipation Proclamation. I was thinking and writing about how people—black and poor—continue to struggle and suffer. I began to write about the color of suffering. I could see it. I could feel it. I could hear Jesus on the cross of Calvary crying, "*Eloi, Eloi, lama sabachthani.*" I, too, felt forsaken. My God, why?

The election of Barack Obama to the pinnacle of American power and prestige has caused me to think about the past, present, and future, especially as they relate to race as a social construction and my life as an African American. In spite of my skepticism, I am very proud of his achievement and hopeful that change will ultimately mean transformation in the sense that Franz Kafka demonstrated in *The Metamorphosis* and Hans Gadamer in *Truth and Method*. And in the sense that Jesus demonstrated in preaching that the oppressed shall be set free (cf. Luke 4:18). If the election of Barack Obama has done nothing else, it has brought to life in my own spirit and soul the words of James Weldon Johnson:

> Sing a song full of the faith that the dark past
>   has taught us,

Sing a song full of the hope that the present has brought us.

Facing the rising sun of our new day begun,
Let us march on till victory is won.

While we have not achieved any ultimate victory relative to freedom, justice, and equality in America, Barack Obama is the embodiment of the hope that the present has brought us.

NOTES

1. See H. Richard Niebuhr, *The Meaning of Revelation* (Louisville: Westminster John Knox, 2006); and Paul Ricoeur, *Interpretation Theory: Discourse and the Surplus of Meaning* (Fort Worth, Tex.: Texas Christian University Press, 1976).

2. Barack Obama, *The Audacity of Hope* (New York: Three Rivers, 2006), 228–30.

3. See Friedrich Wilhelm Nietzsche, *Beyond Good and Evil* (New York: Penguin Putnam, 1973).

4. James Henry Harris, *The Forbidden Word: A Memoir* (unpublished manuscript, 2009).

22
BARACK OBAMA AND
THE AMERICAN CIVIL RELIGION

VALERIE ELVERTON DIXON

If religion is the tie that binds us, a set of values and ideals that unifies us, and faith in an entity that commands our devotion and becomes the object of our ultimate concern, then there is an American civil religion. It exists between citizens and outside of the coercion or authority of established ecclesial or military power. The American civil religion has all the accoutrements of religion. It has its sacred texts, hymns, holy places, holy days, and symbols. It has its gods and goddesses, priests, prophets, heroes, and martyrs. They all touch us to our core. They help us define ourselves and take us to a kind of transcendence, to "a firm reliance on the protection of Divine Providence," and cause us to "mutually pledge to each other our lives, our fortunes and our sacred honor."[1] These concluding words of the Declaration of Independence are the beating heart of the American civil religion. Citizens pledge their lives to one another with faith in a transcendent power.

Barack Obama's run for president was an act of audacious faith in God and in the nation. He intuitively understands the civil religion and is able to articulate a vision of national unity within the context of this tradition. A civil religion, however, can only lead to existential disappointment. The question now becomes, how can this faith lead to an audacious faith that points beyond the nation?

Like all religions, the American civil religion has its sacred texts, both written and oral. The Declaration of Independence, the U.S. Constitution, the Bill of Rights, the *Federalist Papers*, Lincoln's "Gettysburg Address," Franklin Delano Roosevelt's "Four Freedoms," Martin Luther King Jr.'s "I have a dream" speech, and Barack Obama's speech to the Democratic Convention in 2004 are among the texts that comprise the sacred canon of our civil religion. We often sing sacred songs: "America," "Lift Every Voice and Sing," and "God Bless America," and we sing "The Star-Spangled Banner," our national anthem, before most sports events.

We have preserved and constructed sacred places, such as Independence Hall in Philadelphia and the Old North Church of Boston. However, the most sacred space may be the National Mall in Washington, DC. It has been that space where Americans of all political persuasions have come to make a case for their vision of perfecting the Union. Monuments and memorials stand there in silent testimony. We go there to touch and to remember.

The holy days of the civil religion come mainly in the summer—Memorial Day, Independence Day, Labor Day. November brings Thanksgiving. Our sacred symbols include the bald eagle, the Liberty Bell, and the Statue of Liberty. The flag is perhaps our most sacred symbol. When men and women who have served this country die, we present a flag to their families at the gravesite. We offer it with thanks from a grateful nation.

The gods of the nation are nature and nature's God, Divine Providence, the Almighty. During Barack Obama's inauguration, God was articulated in more complex ways. The Rt. Rev. Gene Robinson referred to the God of many understandings. Rev. Joseph Lowery prayed to the God of "our weary years and silent tears." Our goddesses are freedom, Lady Liberty and Justice, the blind goddess.

We honor our martyrs. We remember Abraham Lincoln, John Kennedy, Martin Luther King, Jr., and Robert Kennedy as American saints because they died working to keep America strong and trying to perfect the Union. At the same time, there are millions of heroes and sheroes, known only to a few, who shed blood, sweat, and tears because of their love of country. Radicals who protested racism, war, and inequality in the streets of the United States also stand as patriots.

The civil religion is not established by law. It does not explicitly exist in any of our founding documents. The American civil religion cannot be described as Judeo-Christian. As much as Christians and Christianity are part of our history, the civil religion is of no religious tradition other than itself. To define itself as Christian or Jewish or Judeo-Christian would make every citizen who does not profess these religious traditions, by definition, a second-class citizen. That would violate the liberty and the justice that the country holds as two of its most enduring ideals.

The American civil religion is very close to the civil religion described by Jean-Jacques Rousseau in *The Social Contract*,2 who said a civil religion ought to believe in the existence of "a mighty, intelligent, and beneficent Divinity." The Divinity should be "possessed of foresight and providence." The civil religion should teach that the social contract and the nation's laws are sacred. It should prohibit intolerance. Rousseau's civil religion prohibits intolerance because civil religion cannot be exclusive.

Since the civil religion is not officially established, how does it come into being? In the book *Habits of the Heart*,3 Robert Bellah and his cowriters use a concept found in Alexis de Tocqueville's *Democracy in America*. Habits of the heart are the mores, the moral ecology of a society. These habits spring from a societal consensus about what is right, about what makes a virtuous person and a good citizen. The civil religion holds that the virtue of the nation derives from the virtue of its people. An assault on the virtue of the nation becomes an assault on the virtue of its people. This is why the nation scorns and makes marginal those who preach a prophetic critique. Habits of the heart are formed in family, church, school, and in local and national politics. They are formed in that moral space between what is right for the individual and what is right for larger groups—family, community, and nation.

Bellah and others describe three important strands of America's moral ecology—biblical, republican, and expressive utilitarian individualism. American society wants its nation to conform to the biblical hope of a good society; it wants people to participate as good citizens in the republic; and it wants its citizens to have freedom to express and to enrich themselves.[4] These three strands come together in the American civil religion.

However, like all religions, the American civil religion is dangerous. When a religion stops with faith only in itself—its own gods, texts, and doctrines—it becomes tribalistic and coercive. It wants the entire world to believe as it believes, in the same way it believes. When a religion itself becomes the object of its ultimate concern, it is dangerous. Christian theologian Paul Tillich wrote about the concept of ultimate concern.[5] For Tillich, faith exists when we are ultimately concerned. The object of our ultimate concern subordinates everything else, including our own lives. Faith is an act of will that brings together human rationality and human emotions, allowing human beings to imagine transcendence. Through faith, we see beyond sight and know beyond proof that there is a better day, a better way, a better world in which to live. It is a kind of ecstasy.

The problems come when the object of our ultimate concern is not ultimate. The ultimate thing is both in us and beyond us. It erases the subject-object divide. That which cannot do this, according to Tillich, is not ultimate. He writes: "The finite which claims infinity without having it (as, e.g., a nation or success) is not able to transcend the subject-object scheme. It remains an object which the believer looks at as a subject."[6]

American civil religion is idolatry because it puts faith in a created thing and not in the creator. At the end of the day, idols disappoint. The ecstasy that faith brings becomes existential disappointment when we put our faith in that which is not ultimate. Faith is not static. Faith contains doubt within itself. The opposite forces of faith and doubt, each working with and against the other, create an energy, an intensity that gives life to faith. Faith moves from object to object, each pointing beyond itself to the ultimate. Thus, when we grow content with faith in the nation, we open the door to our own existential disappointment.

the audacity of faith

Barack Obama has demonstrated a genius for articulating the foundational vision of America. While others running for president had a list of policies for the various problems facing the United States, Obama gave the American people a unifying vision of itself that echoed the ideal of *E Pluribus Unum*; from many one. In this regard he assumed the pastor-preacher voice that exhorts us not only to work for personal good, but also to work for the common good. His audacious faith strengthens our own faith and tells us, "Yes, we can," and we believe him. We believe that the impossible is possible for the nation and for our own lives.

Barack Obama preaches American exceptionalism. He reminds us of the uniqueness of the country that would open the doors of opportunity to a black man and elect him president of the United States. On election night, he said: "If there is anyone out there who still doubts that America is a place where all things are possible; who still wonders if the dream of our founders is alive in our time; who still questions the power of our democracy—tonight is your answer."[7] By drawing attention to the work of the people of the United States and calling the election victory our victory, he made the connection between the virtue of the people and the virtue of the country. We all felt good to be American that night.

During the early days of his administration, while facing one of the worst economic crises in American history, two wars, and a Congress that despite Obama's best efforts still follows political ideology rather than clear-eyed pragmatism, Obama spoke of the importance of both individual responsibility and of our responsibilities to one another. At the 102nd Abraham Lincoln Association Annual Dinner in Springfield, Illinois, celebrating the two hundredth birthday of Lincoln, he spoke not only about self reliance, but about the union.

"Only by coming together, all of us, in union, and expressing that sense of shared sacrifice and responsibility—for ourselves, yes, but for one another—can we do the work that must be done in this country. That is part of the definition of being American."[8]

We are living at a critical moment in American history. It is a difficult moment, but it is also a moment of tremendous possibilities.

It is a moment when a new vision of relationship may be born. The nation has elected in Barack Obama an intelligent, elegant, and eloquent man who is secure in the knowledge of his own worth, with or without the presidency. He knows the weight of responsibility the nation has placed upon him. He is the priest-president of the American civil religion. However, the civil religion will leave us in a state of existential disappointment unless it points beyond itself to something more ultimate, more absolute, and more infinite. This is beyond Barack Obama's eloquence. It is beyond his presidential power.

We ought to deploy our own audacious faith and allow it to take us beyond our moral ecology and habits of the heart, beyond our civil religion, and beyond our own religious traditions to a radical love that prays God's blessing not only on America, but on all of creation, even on our enemies. Such an audacious faith is ours to believe. Such a radical love is our love to love.

NOTES

1. Jack N. Rakove, ed., *Founding America: Documents from the Revolution to the Bill of Rights* (New York: Barnes and Noble, 2006).

2. Jean-Jacques Rousseau, *The Social Contract and Discourses* (London: Orion, 1999).

3. Robert N. Bellah, Richard Madsen, William M. Sullivan, Ann Swidler, and Steven M. Tipton, *Habits of the Heart: Individualism and Commitment in American Life* (Berkeley: University of California Press, 1985).

4. Ibid., 28.

5. Paul Tillich, *Dynamics of Faith* (New York: HarperCollins, 2001).

6. Ibid., 13.

7. Barack Obama, "This Is Your Victory," *Rolling Stone*, Commemorative Edition, 2008, 126.

8. Barack Obama, "Remarks by the President at the 102nd Abraham Lincoln Association Annual Banquet," http://www.whitehouse.gov/the_press_office/ Remarks-by-the-President-at-the-102nd-Abraham-Lincoln-Association-Annual-Banquet (accessed February 21, 2009).

23
OBAMA'S RACE AND AMERICA'S RACE RELATIONS

DWIGHT N. HOPKINS

Since the November 4, 2008, presidential elections, I have been receiving congratulatory e-mails hailing the new racial, ethnic, and global era ushered in by President Barack Obama. Close friends, professional colleagues, and casual acquaintances throughout the United States and across the world have written me and claimed Obama as the son of their state, their country, or their region of the globe. Of course, countless black Americans have written articles and "burned up" cyberspace with shouts of joy. Finally, in the passionate logic of African Americans, "in our lifetime one of us is in the White House."

How is it possible that Hawaii owns Obama as theirs? Indonesia and parts of Asia perceive him as reflecting their experiences. Kenya screams in ecstasy to have a blood relative at 1600 Pennsylvania Avenue. All of Africa embraces him as a close kin of that continent. Kansans believe his roots sink deep within their soil. And black Americans, without much critical self-reflection, relish in a taken-for-granted jubilation that the forty-fourth president is black like them.

That Obama is perceived in a variety of ways as belonging to such disparate audiences indicates, at least, one salient point about race relations in America—the absurdity of the "one-drop rule."

Coming out of slavery and segregation, the one-drop rule was one of the most egregious public policy perspectives based on the institution of white supremacy. When Africans arrived in chains to the thirteen colonies, all of their children were forced to be called black even if the biological parent was a white man or a white woman. If it was determined that a white person had any African or black ancestors, that white person was reclassified as black. "One drop" of black blood in one's genealogy could instantly transfer a white citizen into a black nightmare.

The corollary to the one-drop rule is its eventual acceptance by all black Americans. For instance, Walter White, a pioneer leader of the NAACP, was so white looking that he once attended a high-society function and some of the whites present murmured about why he brought his light-skinned "black" wife. The irony of the situation was that White was actually "black." And his so-called light-skinned black wife was actually "white"!

The one-drop-of-black-blood rule is, seemingly, a unique American mythology. It presupposes that the United States is a black-white paradigm. One extreme is "white" people. The other extreme is "black" people. In between black and white, placed in subordinated status, are the beautiful kaleidoscope of Asian Americans, Caribbean Americans, African Americans, Pacific Island Americans, Hispanic Americans, Middle-Eastern Americans, European Americans, and American Indians (the first people of the land). A white person is kicked out of the white extreme when someone discloses his or her past one drop of black blood. That person is then relegated to the black extreme. And all the colors in between the two polarities are expected to take sides.

The absurdity of the one-drop rule is shown, by eminent Harvard scholar Henry "Skip" Gates's two-part TV series, in which he traces the genetic background of famous "black" academics, artists, and activists. Many of them discover that they are descendants of "white" people. Similarly, scientists have shown that there is more genetic commonality between "blacks and whites" than there are among "blacks." So the categories "white" and "black" are created by human beings. The one-drop rule seems to have an American particularity. In other parts of the world we encounter a more fluid definition of race. For example, Asians in England are often allowed to be called black.

What race is Obama? Shortly after the November 4 election, the venerable Congressman John Lewis (Georgia) said that no black person who had come out of segregation and the civil rights movement could have been elected the first black president. His conclusion rings true.

Obama redefines what it means to be "black." His ancestors do not come from the glorious West African empires of centuries ago. To my knowledge, he has no biological connection to those people's evil encounter with the European slave trade. His family history flows not from *de jure* and *de facto* segregation. He literally was living in Asia and the Pacific Islands during the civil rights, black power, pan-African, and reparations efforts impacting the forty-eight contiguous states of America. He has never lived in the (segregated or nonsegregated) southern United States. In his major speeches, he doesn't mention by name two heroic icons of black manhood—Martin Luther King Jr. and Malcolm X. Rather, we more often hear references to Abraham Lincoln and, to a lesser degree, Franklin D. Roosevelt. Obama was not born into nor did he grow up in a black church. No wonder he did not assemble black preacher leaders and civil rights stalwarts together and, from that base, launch his presidential campaign.

Obama is Hawaiian and Pacific Island—flip-flops, surfing, snorkeling, Aloha Spirit, and Ohana family values. Before living in the segregated Chicago black community, his material reality was Asia and the Pacific. Born in Hawaii in 1961, he matured with other Hawaiian citizens—Japanese Hawaiians, Chinese Hawaiians, Filipino Hawaiians, Pacific Island Hawaiians, native Hawaiians, and white Hawaiians. The black-white paradigm of the mainland did not exist during his years there. In fact, whites were, and still are, a minority. And blacks were, and still are, a rarity. Most are Waikiki visitors on vacation and those stationed temporarily on military bases.

Obama is somewhat socialized Indonesian and Southeast Asian. He spent ages six to ten in Indonesia, going to school and speaking their language. His Indonesian stepfather gave him an ape as a pet. This pet was not caged, but lived in their backyard.

Obama was nurtured "white." His Kansas white mother (not from the South) reared him in a white culture with his white grandparents. (And all accounts indicate that no black men or women, boys or girls ever lived in his home until he married and then had his own children.) He perceived his grandmother, perhaps, as a white transplant to Hawaii. Unlike most black Americans who call their grandmothers Big Mama, Ma Dear, or Grand Ma, Obama's intimate name for his white grandmother is Toot—the Hawaiian endearment for grandmother.

Obama has never self-identified as an Afrocentric person or as pan-Africanist. But actually he is probably more African than the overwhelming majority of black Americans. There is no mystery that requires him to do a genetic test to find out what West African "tribe" his ancestors came from centuries ago. Actually, he is not from the African West Coast. He is Kenyan—East African. His father voluntarily came to the United States in 1959, not in chains in 1619 to Jamestown, Virginia. Father Obama was formerly a goat herder in Kenya. President Obama literally has immediate relatives there. He knows how to find and can visit the exact location where his father and other ancestors were born. He understands what his "tribal" language, politics, economics, religions, foods, songs, indigenous names, folktales, clothing, dances, illnesses, personalities, and grave sites are. When he pours libations (i.e., spills liquids on the ground in memory of dead ones), he is not talking about unknown Africans lost in the slave trade. Like Africans on the continent, he would pour libations to his specific blood family members. And he, like those Africans, would pour them on their family grave sites. Some of those burial grounds are still next to family compounds in Kenya. And Obama doesn't have to change his English slave master's name to an African one. He already has an African name, because he, like his father, is Kenyan.

After about twenty-two years of this socialization, Obama came to the intensely segregated South Side of Chicago. There, for the first time in a sustained manner, he engaged the traditional black-white paradigm and one-drop rule. Segregated Chicago offered him three things—a black family through marriage, a black community through grassroots organizing, and a black church through baptism. This is not to say that he was unaware of the mainland's obsession with race. It is not to say he didn't know that he was black, among other realities. Witness his Afro hairstyle at Punahou, one of the most elite private schools in the United States. And his idolizing of "Dr. J" of the National Basketball Association's Philadelphia 76ers attests to his knowledge as well.

Still Barack Obama symbolizes that something has changed in America. History will judge whether his movement signifies a qualitative or quantitative racial reconfiguration. Maybe we will begin to see the following. If he doesn't redefine race in America, Obama will expand what race means. Perhaps he will help the millions of Americans with black and white parents, black and Asian parents, and black and Hispanic parents integrate the tugging of their identities—identities that force them into only one racial option. Who knows? Will a white person with black blood finally be able to remain white?

The forty-fourth president of the United States is American. Like all citizens, this Hawaiian, Polynesian, Indonesian, Asian, white, Kenyan, and black human being is caught up in the narrative of the black-white paradigm—a structure still rooted in the absurdity of the one-drop-of-black-blood rule. Yes, he is black. But no one can deeply understand him unless he or she appreciates the rainbow ethnic mixtures of Hawaii.

24
POSTRACE AMERICA

A. ROY MEDLEY

The convergence of the Martin Luther King Jr. holiday and the inauguration of Barack Obama as president of the United States marked a turning point in American history. That turning point was more than just perception—it was a reality rooted in the election of America's first African American president by a broad base that included sizable sectors of every major racial/ethnic group in the country. His election is a tribute to how the social consciousness of the country was changed by the courage and convictions of Dr. King and countless others, such as Rosa Parks, Viola Liuzzo, Hosea Williams, Clarence Jordan, Medgar Evers, and James Reeb. For those of us who were privileged to live through the 1960s and now witness this moment, there is a profound sense of joy and wonder that this day has come to pass in our lifetime.

Obama's election jolted many who had predicted that America would not elect a black president—at least not now—because racism was too entrenched. And it has thrown the whole calculation of "race" in our culture into a tailspin. Howard Thurman penned, "The burden of being black and the burden of being white is so heavy that it is rare in our society to experience oneself as a human being." However, on November 4, many felt that weighty reality shed for a moment. Oprah's head perched on the shoulder of a white man as Obama accepted his election is an icon of that moment.

Has racism ended with this one election? Certainly not, but it would be unfair and untrue to ignore the hopeful changes taking place in America. First, while those of us who grew up before or during the civil rights era still bear many of the scars and wounds of the horrors of forced segregation in the South and de facto segregation in the North, there is a younger generation for whom this is not their reality. They have come of age with heroes and heroines, pop culture stars and TV anchors, and politicians and sports figures of many different colors and cultures. Theirs is a more multihued universe than was the case for earlier generations of Americans.

Second, there is an increase of cross-racial/cross-cultural marriages, the children of which live a reality that is represented in Obama, Tiger Woods, and many others who own their multiple heritages. I still recall our neighbor's children of a decade ago complaining about the check boxes for race on surveys and forms where the only categories were the traditional White, Black, Hispanic, Asian, and Native American—none of which fully described who they were. Their reality, in which one heritage was not suppressed in favor of the other, but in which each was fully embraced for who they were, is a relatively new phenomenon in our country.

Third, American society is far more multiracial and multicultural than it was in the 1960s. While the relationship between blacks and whites has long been the center of the discussion about diversity in America (even last year's New Baptist Covenant gathering in Atlanta reflected this bilateral definition of diversity), immigration patterns that began in the 1970s have reshaped this nation's identity. While for some that is a frightening reality, for many others it is a welcome enrichment of our lives. We no longer have to define ourselves over and against others but can discover our identity in community with them.

As the face of our country to the world and to ourselves, Obama, who honors both his black and his white ancestry and who has come of age in post-segregation America, has the opportunity to help us live into the new reality King and others opened for us— the reality of an America where color does not define privilege or position; it just is.

25

BODIES—AMERICAN MADE
The 2008 Presidential Election and the Possibility of a New Politics of Race

ANTHONY B. PINN

Civil rights struggles of the twentieth century brought new sociopolitical structures of life, meaning, and opportunities. The civil rights movement meant more than changed laws and policies, more than revision to the explicit structures and discourses of conduct and perception that guide these United States. No, the civil rights rhetoric pushed for a rethinking of the manner in which race, gender, and class shape our bodies—how these bodies are represented, "read," and organized in time and space. This, I believe, is what Dr. Martin L. King Jr. expressed in his call for attention to the "content of our character" over against the stereotyping of our bodies as the litmus test for judgment of our value.

As inspiring and transformative as was that push for equality during the mid-twentieth century, it did not serve to break the back of discrimination based on appearance. Black bodies continued to be attacked and stigmatized. We would have to wait some forty years after the assassination of Martin L. King Jr. before the call for new standards of value and worth—a new framing of human integrity—would give rise to perhaps one of the most substantial signs of progress in our collective history: the election of an African American to the presidency of the United States of America.

The graceful presence of Barack Obama on the platform in Chicago accepting the call from an overwhelming percentage of U.S. citizens to lead us into a new and more productive mode of life responded to the imaginings offered by King: "I have a dream that my four little children will one day live in a nation where they will not be judged by the color of their skin but by the content of their character."[1] At that point in Chicago, after so many years of struggle, it appeared the United States would finally live up to its potential and recognize the merit of its people based on the strength of their intellect, their drive, their determination, and the appeal of their vision. This sense of hopefulness, the push toward the capturing of a promise, found more affirmation in the inaugural activities of January 20, 2009: *President* Barack Obama.

It is only reasonable that Obama's decisive victory would raise speculations concerning the end of racial discrimination: Does not an African American president mark the demise of white supremacy, of intolerance and racial fear? Is this the mark of a completed task, the transformation of the United States into a nation marked by tolerance, equality, and creative diversity? Have we as a nation brought concluding truth to the sentiment of the haunting song penned years ago by James Weldon Johnson?

> Stony the road we trod,
> Bitter the chast'ning rod,
> Felt in the days when hope unborn had died;
> Yet with a steady beat,
> Have not our weary feet
> Come to the place for which our fathers sighed?
> We have come over a way that with tears
>   has been watered,
> We have come, treading our path through the blood
>   of the slaughtered,
> Out from the gloomy past,
> Till now we stand at last
> Where the white gleam of our bright star is cast.[2]

From black bodies hanging as "strange fruit" on trees, to the black body as marker of political leadership at the highest level, U.S. popular imagination and perspective(s) on race have undergone a radical shift. But is this the end of the story, a reason to believe we are now in a postrace phase of our nation's existence?

My answer will displease some: No. What is more, the question above—Are we now a postrace nation?—asked by so many over the course of the past several months is wrongheaded. It is ideologically fixed and socially reified, wed to a denial of difference as a positive, a necessary marker of our nation's complexity. It is the sign of an old discourse of American-ness that lacks the stuff of rich and layered relationships and denies the human geographies that mark the cartography of our collective existence. More to the point, efforts to answer yes to the question of a postrace nation fail to recognize a fundamental reality: we exist as embodied realities, and this embodiment must be recognized, celebrated, and incorporated into the workings of our national existence.

Our bodies, as sociologists and philosophers have remarked, are both biochemical realities and symbols of the social system. That is to say, on one level our bodies are constructed through discourse and given meaning through what we believe about them in line with our worldviews. For example, during the period of slavery, black bodies were constructed as markers of depravity, danger, and white superiority. And the symbolic body so constructed was used to justify and reinforce the patterns that marked U.S. life. The black physical body was seen as different in a negative manner, as less aesthetically pleasing than white bodies, and by extension of less value and importance. Hence, it could be used, abused, and destroyed without consequence. This pattern of behavior toward blacks had nothing to do with any true difference between physical white and black bodies. Rather, it had to do with social rules and regulations that were painted onto these physical bodies.

Bodies matter because "meaning, in short, resides in the body, and the body resides in the world."[3] Bodies are read, and this process shapes our interactions, our relationships...our politics, and our political activities.

What I am suggesting is rather simple. Much of what we "know" or believe about groups of humans is premised on what we believe about their bodies. In fact, our institutions, beliefs, and practices are understood in relationship to the presentation and activities of our bodies. And society—its rules and regulations, the ordering of our social existence—involves the controlling of how bodies occupy time and space; and this is graphically present in the history of black bodies in the United States, from slavery to the present.[4]

We should not be so naive as to believe the election of Barack Obama marks the end of racism. November 5 and January 20 did not find our nation free of hatred and inequality. We have reached a moment of great potential, but one that is firmly lodged in a situation of great need. Discrimination based on color, gender, sexual orientation, age, class, and so on remains a challenge. We as a nation continue to exist below the horizon of our rhetoric of greatness. Fixing this problem, however, does not require a denial of our differences. There is no need to reject the diversity of our nation.

I fear that lurking behind the dream of a color-blind society is an effort to normalize all groups consistent with the sensibilities and "marking" of the largest segment of the population—white Americans. Such a move involves an implied effort to render all bodies in the image of white bodies—to make comfortable the status quo by reading all members of our society in light of the status quo. This type of arrangement, as should be clear, fails to provide a strong challenge to white supremacy and does not push our nation to live out the best of its democratic principles and values.

President Obama marks in body and outlook the complex and diverse nature of U.S. history and life. Drawing into one frame the expansive interconnectedness of the world, he signals the collective reality of our "thick" existence, the interrelated nature of the "stuff" of American life. It is my hope that in selecting Barack Obama, U.S. citizens have demanded a shift with respect to how bodies are read and in the availability of equal opportunities for all. Yet this does not mean bodies are no longer racialized, that we no longer see color on bodies. What is more, there is no reason it should mean the emergence of a race-blind society. We need and should want better than that. Instead, what the election of Barack Obama should encourage is an appreciation of diversity, of difference, as a marker of our strength.

It would not benefit us to deny our differences; doing so would truncate our strengths and render myopic our view of the future. When you see President Obama, see a black man and recognize the history associated with his physical and metaphorical black body. Doing so is vital, and to avoid doing so is to dismiss the layered nature of our history, to dismiss the mosaic that is the true nature of the United States. But also recognize the manner in which his body is not all there is; recognize the manner in which the weight of the dreams and desires for this country have been borne by a host of bodies—all of them vital and vibrant, all of them representing something of what is beautiful and vital about our nation.

A race-blind society? No. A better marker of our potential as a nation, a better sign of our commitment to change, is an honest embrace of our differences as a fundamental strength. For far too long the boast of U.S. greatness has been rhetorically engaging but ground in consistent acts of greatness. Finally, through this election, we have begun—not concluded—a process of anchoring our hopefulness in action and in the embrace of all people who call this land "home." We have set out new opportunities for engagement, a truly shared sense of ownership over the future of this nation.

A new grammar of difference is in the making; a new sense of our potential and purpose is possible; but we have much work to do before our hope is fixed in a new reality. The true manifestation of our democratic vision is not the occupancy of the White House by an African American, but proper housing for all, healthy life options for all, economic security for all, protection of our shared natural environment, and the restoration of all the other diminished dimensions of our shared existence. President Obama is a sign of our movement in the direction of a new United States, but only a sign, not the promised fulfilled. The latter depends on all of us.

NOTES

1. Martin L. King Jr., "I Have a Dream" speech.
2. James Weldon Johnson, "Lift Every Voice and Sing."
3. Simon J. Williams and Gillian Bendelow, *The Lived Body: Sociological Themes, Embodied Issues* (New York: Routledge, 1998), 54.
4. Ibid., 25, 65.

26
THIS IS OUR WORK

VALERIE BRIDGEMAN

The United States presidential election of 2008 brought a mix of emotions, but for the most part, both in this country and around the world, people could be heard and seen celebrating this historic moment. Some of those who celebrated now believe that the United States has finally made good on its promise that "all people are created equal." People descended from or akin to dusky skin tones saw someone who looked like them ascend to this nation's highest office. There was dancing in the streets.

I happened to be in Chicago on the night before the election. During the cab ride to the airport, my driver, a native of Saudi Arabia, was giddy. "I am not a citizen of this country," he said with the thickest of accents, "but I am so happy! I know that we, that you will elect this man, Mr. Obama!" He beamed. I asked him why he was so excited. And this was his answer: "When hope is alive and the right leader is in place, things can change in a minute. The world will be happy and love America again," he said. "I pray for him every day," he continued. "I pray that these mean people will not harm him, because I believe he is the best hope for this world."

What powerful imagery—the hope that a man, a symbol of sorts, can change the world. The cab driver's language and the tenor of his voice were reverent, as if the discussion was about a messianic figure. I remember thinking that this Saudi Arabian cab driver believed much more than I did in the possibility of the change that could come with Obama's election.

This statement might sound as if I am a cynic, but I am not. What I am is a student and a witness of United States culture and history.

I lived through the 1960s and 1970s—some of this nation's most difficult transitions since the Civil War and post-Reconstruction. I remember when schools were integrated in central Alabama; and I remember when the school my siblings and friends had attended for so long, the one I was to attend—Phyllis Wheatley High School—had its name changed because white parents did not want their children to attend a school named after a black woman.

So my hope about what is possible with the election of Barack Obama as president of the United States of America was tempered by my own memories and to some extent by the scars I bear from growing up in the racist Deep South. I wanted to believe and be as jubilant as my cab driver. I wanted to be able to "forget what was behind and press toward this [new] mark," but something constrained me from sharing in his jubilant expectation.

These are wonderful and horrible times. The hope expressed in the vote for Barack Obama testifies to the fact that this country is in that vortex of change, that time when seismic shifts occur in caldrons of elation and violence. And so in the wake of this change, the fissures of our national soul are not subtle. This historic election has exposed gaping wounds, historical hurts, and a painful past. It has also exposed systemic struggles that inscribed oppression and violence, dehumanizing laws, and immoral social practices into the fabric of American life. We are reminded of this pain even as we celebrate, because we live in the 24/7 news cycle, in the era of YouTube and Facebook, Twitter and camera phones. We find ourselves swimming in the nonstop chatter of CNN and MSNBC. The sheer volume of news cycles and news channels is both numbing and unnerving. We are bombarded and seduced by such hype.

Faith-filled people—that is, spiritual or religious people of all traditions—are just as seduced by these frantic times. We want to believe. We hope against hope. We pray for President Obama as we pray for a savior—"Even so, come." Like my cab driver, many people often speak of President Obama with messianic undertones—a once and future leader like David, the ideal biblical leader. We want President Obama to lead us, to take care of us, to fix everything that is broken in this country and in the world. We want him to provide us with security of both wealth and body. In a twist on Zora Neale Hurston's book *Their Eyes Were Watching God*, "our eyes are watching Barack Obama." Many of us have elevated our president and this nation-state to an idolatrous station, and in doing so we have built altars to the government that are no less problematic for us than for those who lived in the sixth century BCE during Jeremiah's times, on the cusp of the Babylonian exile.

We have this uneasy tension. On the one hand, there are those people who are weary of the quest for liberation and justice for everyone. For that group, still popping champagne corks and partying "like it's 1999," the racial past was erased with one glorious election. For them, our racial problems are done and our international image is restored. For them, God has provided a healing, a crossing of a new Jordan, deliverance once and for all. The attitude on that side is "Sit back and watch as 'our man' works his magic."

On the other hand, there are those who, while they believe God's hand moved in this election in some way to work toward justice, also live with a low-grade dread that the ugliness of racial animosity just under the surface will rear its ugly head once again. This group believes that the soul of this nation has been exposed as being weak, sick, distorted, and in some quarters, demonic. There are many people who do not believe the election "proved" we are a postracial society, but rather that we harbor a virulent racism that is unhealed and unresolved. That unresolved sickness showed itself in the chanting of second and third graders, "Assassinate Obama!" on a bus in Maryland.[1] It manifested itself in a betting pool where people could wager on when the new president would be killed.[2] It showed up in a picture making the rounds on the Internet of watermelons on the lawn of the White House in lieu of the annual Easter egg hunt.[3]

Has the United States become a postracial society? Hardly! We have an oozing, deeply infected national wound that some people have struggled to heal, but which many others have been content to cover with a bandage. Christians and people of other faiths as well have been at the vanguard of the struggle to heal this wound, but sometimes we have only "healed the hurt of the nation carelessly, saying, 'Peace, peace,'" (Jeremiah 8:11) when there has been only a tenuous truce. We have chanted, sung, and hummed, "Yes, we can." We have replayed the will.i.am song on YouTube.

We should celebrate for how far this nation has come, but we must not assume that the work of justice has been completed. We must not yell, "Peace," where people may publicly use derogatory racial terms and mete out violence. We must not cry, "Peace," in a violent culture, a warmongering nation, a sin-sick society where poverty prevails in the wealthiest nation on earth. We are not yet saved. We have had and must continue to have a season of celebration, but we must not be content to lean on a human shoulder and settle for slight healing. God's intent for this nation, for all nations, and indeed for all creation is shalom.

We are called to this work of shalom in the face of our own exiles. We have been summoned by the God of Jeremiah not only to name these sins, but also to lend our lives to the pursuit of justice and shalom. We have been called to pray for President Obama, but never to believe that he is the sole answer to this world's or this country's problems. That would make him God. And he is not God. We have been called to continue to work toward real healing, deep healing, divine healing of deep divides—to continue to pray for and sweat for the eradication of the "isms" that are the ooze of the wounds of this country, indeed of the world—wounds that give witness to human sin. This is the work of God's people. It is the work of God. And while we pray for President Obama and thank God for any role his leadership may play in bringing about the changes my Saudi cab driver was expecting, we must surely know that if we do not join the Holy One in repairing the world, our celebration will be in vain. For as Psalm 127:1 says, "Unless the LORD builds the house, those who build it labor in vain."

NOTES

1. http://www.2news.tv/news/local/34274374.html (accessed March 17, 2009).
2. http://www.msnbc.msn.com/id/27724965/ (accessed March 17, 2009).
3. http://www.huffingtonpost.com/2009/02/25/white-house-watermelon-em_n _169933.html (accessed March 17, 2009).

27

BARACK OBAMA AND THE NEW AMERICAN CIVIL RELIGION
Official Version

LEONARD SWEET

For the world has changed, and we must change with it.
—Barack Obama[1]

Barack Obama is the first Google president. All the presidents before him were Gutenberg presidents, the products of a print culture and the high priests of a civil religion that was print based and all that went with that technology. The forty-fourth president is the product of a very different world, a digital, electronic culture, and his transitional and transformational presidency is already shaping the contours of a post-Gutenberg, Google culture civil religion. Barack Obama is pioneering a new American Civil Religion—Official Version, if you will, a new ACROV.[2]

In the case of USAmerica, the "official version" of American civil religion was shaped primarily by the Jeffersonian Creed of liberty, equality, democracy, civil rights, nondiscrimination, the rule of law, and the tenets of Protestant faith.[3] It is my conviction that ACROV is being transitioned and transformed from a Gutenberg to a Google paradigm with the presidency of Barack Obama.

The Gutenberg world is most often known as "modernity,"[4] which was inaugurated by the invention of the printing press, accelerated with the scientific revolution that began in the sixteenth century, was in full swing with the eighteenth-century Enlightenment, and crested with the Industrial Revolution, which dominated the nineteenth and early twentieth centuries.

The Google world, sometimes known as "postmodernity,"[5] was inaugurated by the invention of the cell phone (1973), which today is no longer primarily a "phone" among its 3.3 billion users (that's half the population of planet Earth), but a communications and learning center, with almost instant access to the accumulated wisdom of the ages. Compare the social environment of a child born in 1950, or even 1970, with the social environment of a child born today. We're not even on the same planet. Ten years ago half of humanity had never made a phone call and only 20 percent of humanity had regular access to communications. For the first time in history, the majority of humanity is connected.

This short essay will explore three prominent features of the new ACROV as manifested in the presidential inauguration in the tone and texture of the sacred speech known as the "inaugural address."

THIS IS A GLOBAL ACROV

Obama is our first postracial, postcolonial president. With a father from Kenya, a mother from Kansas, and a childhood in Indonesia, Obama is an African American who grew up with an identity not Southern but cosmopolitan and multicultural.

Postracial and Cosmopolitan In the urban ACROV, hybrid and multiple affiliations are increasingly the norm. As of 2008, the majority of the world's population live in cities for the first time in twenty thousand years. USAmerica's largest cities are fast becoming "minority majorities," as minority populations have become majorities. Forty-eight percent of new USAmericans are Hispanic. The average USAmerican is now brown-eyed, brown-skinned, and black-haired, and isn't "melting" but "overcoating."

If you watched the Obama inauguration, you saw cameras panning cheering crowds around the world. From the Bahamas to Botswana, people cheered the inauguration of this forty-fourth president as if he were their own. Obama's inaugural address did not disappoint them: it was ostensibly and dramatically a speech for the whole world, as Obama spent a significant amount of time addressing the peoples of the world.[6] Right after the address, I was listening to *The Ed Schultz Show* ("Where America comes to talk"), and a caller from overseas wanted to speak his mind: "The only thing that could happen bigger than Barack's [*sic*] election to the presidency," he intoned, "is the second coming of Jesus."

This may be the greatest achievement of Barack Obama in the new ACROV: he is giving people a heart that is able to beat across the world. He is the world's first global president.

Socially and Environmentally Responsible The paradox of America's founding is this: no nation was conceived with such high hopes, even millennial dreams about creating the kingdom of God on earth, the perfect society; and yet no nation was conceived with more pillaging and plundering, raping of people and place, looting of gold, silver, and other natural resources. In a global world, militarism is irrelevant to the threat to our nation coming from shrinking ice caps, rising waters, burning deserts, exploding populations, spreading famine, and the like. It is a global world where, for the first time in human history, people sixty-five and older will outnumber children under age five (by 2030), and a graying world requires greening.

Obama is approaching the environmental health movement as the civil rights movement of our times. Our fragile planet is headed toward environmental meltdown if we don't begin to connect ecology and eschatology, not as people with "dominion" over the Earth, but as "trustees" of God's estate. In Obama's theology, God isn't at work destroying the earth; God is at work restoring and redeeming all of creation. The religious witness is about uniting heaven and earth, not separating them.

Transparent Politics is performance, but in the new ACROV a performance art that specializes in transparency, authenticity, and participation. In fact, politics under Obama may be better defined as a *participation* art than a *performance* art.

At the Googleplex, Google's corporate headquarters, there is this saying about transparency: "Ultimately everybody will find out everything." This is true both physically—as high-resolution imagery is removing all secrecy from everyone[7]—and morally—as throne rooms and smoke-filled boardrooms can no longer hide their smoking guns. Obama's transparency (one of his favorite words) is manifest in everything from a budget that does not tuck away or camouflage its most contentious expenditures,[8] to a new presidential style that is casual, loose, cool, humorous, off-the-cuff, colloquial, and honest: "I screwed up."[9]

Postcolonial The American Empire is coming to an end. In the old ACROV, USAmerican foreign policy was self-interested, expansionist, and imperialistic, dedicated to the opening of markets and minds for the expansion of our economy and ideals. The Bush doctrines of preemptive war and full-spectrum dominance pushed the imperial presidency to its furthest reaches.

Just before he died in 2005, political scientist and historian George Kennan started gaining favor again after he lost his influence inside the Beltway in the mid-1950s. Why? Kennan started preaching that the USAmerican needed to attend to "self-perfection" and "spiritual distinction" instead of exporting itself to the rest of the world. Kennan critiqued the USAmerican tendency to see itself as the pinnacle of enlightenment and as a "beacon of truth" to the benighted rest of the world.[10]

This does not mean that the new ACROV is any less interested in making the USAmerican stronger or its people more prosperous, or in evangelizing its ideals of democracy and freedom. But it does mean that there is a new sense of mutuality and reciprocity in our relationships with other nations and cultures.

THIS IS A DIGITAL ACROV

The Associated Press was the quickest to name Obama our first "wired" president. However, that he was not the first to see the potential of the Web. John McCain raised $5.6 million via the Internet and secured more than 130,000 e-mail addresses of supporters. So, too, did George Bush, Al Gore, and Bill Bradley employ the Web in their bids for the presidency. Antonin Scalia, one of the most influential judges in USAmerican history, has twice suggested that he would turn to a television character named Jack Bauer (24) to resolve legal questions about torture, which reflects the unprecedented influence of media on public policy.[11]

But Obama was the first to see the Web with Google goggles. Broadcast media (radio, TV, newspaper) is one-way communication. Social media (blogs, microblogs like Twitter or Facebook) is two-way communication. The only forms of broadcast media that are doing well are those that have reinvented themselves for a Google world, where excellence is not in the quality of the performance but in the quality of the participation (e.g., reality TV, talk radio, local neighborhood rags, etc.).[12]

Obama developed a 13 million-name e-mail list, not primarily to raise money, but to build a relationship with everyone on that list. In fact, Obama's stated reluctance to give up his beloved BlackBerry is because he wants to enable his supporters to feel a personal connection with him and to connect with people outside the Beltway Bubble.[13] Obama understands that if he is to be granted boundless credit by the bank of public opinion, he must encourage participation at all levels of decision making.

Just as print was the primary delivery system in a Gutenberg world, the Internet is now the primary delivery system. In a "wiki culture," every advance has a public collaborative workspace that needs care and feeding. In an attempt to be the first "YouTube president," Obama encouraged the public to watch campaign videos on YouTube. (They watched 15 million hours of them.)[14] Obama promised to bring blogs, vlogs, microblogs, wikis, and other social networking tools into the executive branch, and he even promised to appoint a digital czar for Government 2.0 and his digital presidency. One of the first things Obama did as president was to release a Web video address.

THIS IS A POST-CHRISTIAN ACROV

In a Christendom culture, Christianity flows through the bloodstream of a people; it pulses in their hearts. But USAmerica is finally catching up with Europe in its post-Protestant,[15] post-Christian, increasingly anti-Christian posture. Even Southern culture, once a big sticky glob of competing Christian cultures, is being de-Christianized, with only a thin veneer left coating the culture like the slimy surfaces coating collard greens and okra. In the words of Callum Brown: "It took several centuries...to convert Britain to Christianity, but it has taken less than forty years for the country to forsake it."[16] The spiritual topography of ACROV will increasingly use non-Christian, and perhaps even nonreligious symbols to convey its shared values and promote unity.

The religious autobiography of Barack Obama is a case study of this post-Christian ACROV. His father, stepfather, brother, and grandfather were Muslims, and his name, Barack, means "blessed" in Arabic ("Baruch" means "blessed" in Hebrew). His mother was a disillusioned Methodist who was deeply spiritual but most of all a skeptic about organized religion.[17] As a child, Obama attended a Catholic school and then a Muslim school. Later he was drawn to the writings of Malcolm X, and especially to the Malcolm X philosophy of "by any means necessary." With this pluralist background, Obama has great potential to appeal to the universal *homo religiosus* that lies behind all religious belief and honors the diversity of religious experience, as ACROV shifts from a Western religion to a global expression of common faith.

Even though African Christianity is the shape of things to come for the future of Christianity, if Obama had been more of a black preacher and not the motivational "Yes, we can" speaker that specialized in the power of yes[18] and the lure of the far horizon, he may not have been elected, so strong is this post-Christendom shift in a Google world.

In the old civil religion, to say "I am an American" was to say willy-nilly "I am a Christian." Just as the English poet Percy Bysshe Shelley liked to claim that "we are all Greeks," in some sense the old civil religion made us able to say, "We are all Christians." That old civil religion, thanks to its association with concepts like democracy, liberty, republicanism, and the opportunity to pursue dreams, gave the very word *America* a positive charge.

Because of superpower arrogance, corporate greed, corrupt politics, trigger-happy warmongering, thrusting foreign policy, ecological irresponsibility, and crass consumerism, that very same civil religion gave the name America less happy associations. In fact, just after 9/11, I was asked to speak to some groups in Pretoria and Johannesburg, South Africa. One afternoon before I gave an address to a South African seminary audience, one of the professors stood up from his lofty perch in the back row of the science hall, announced he was taking a moment of personal privilege, and spoke these words: "I hate Americans. I am here because I was told I had to be here by the dean. But I don't know what any American could say that could ever be of interest to me or to any of us in South Africa." Before he sat down, he turned around so the crowd could see both the front and the back of his Osama bin Laden T-shirt.

The question of the new civil religion is whether it will enable people of a Google culture to say:

> I am a USAmerican.
> I am a "Christian/Muslim/Jew/Hindu/nonbeliever."[19]
> I am a citizen of the world.

NOTES

1. Barack Obama, "We Will Remake America," Inauguration Address, January 20, 2009, *Vital Speeches of the Day 75* (February 2009): 52.

2. Conor Cruise O'Brien, in his *The Long Affair: Thomas Jefferson and the French Revolution, 1785–1800* (Chicago: University of Chicago Press, 1996), 318, is the author of this acronym ACROV. For an excellent initial pass at this subject, see the Pew Forum article by Daniel Burke, "Obama Refashions America's Old-Fashioned (Civil) Religion," http://pewforum.org/news/ display.php?NewsID=17365.

3. Samuel P. Huntington, *Who Are We? The Challenge to America's National Identity* (New York: Simon and Schuster, 2004).

4. Some define the phrase "early modern" as extending from the Renaissance to the close of the eighteenth century, taking in the beginning of the Industrial Revolution.

5. For more on this, see Heath White, *Postmodernism 101: The First Course for Curious Christians* (Grand Rapids: Brazos, 2006), and my collection of essays, *The Church of the Perfect Storm* (Nashville: Abingdon, 2008), especially the first chapter, "Outstorming Christianity's Perfect Storm," 1–36.

6. Obama, "We Will Remake America," 50–52. In paragraph 11, Obama begins addressing the peoples of the world with "To the Muslim world..." and

then chooses specific categories of people like "To the people of poor nations…" (Note that the phrase "to the" occurs eight times in the speech!)

7. In Britain, for example, there are 4.2 million CCTV cameras—one for every fifteen people, making it a global third behind China and Malaysia in terms of surveillance. Since the cameras were installed in earnest six years ago, the reported crimes in England have risen and the cleanup rate has fallen. In 2004 Melbourne dismantled its CCTV network, citing its ineffectiveness in preventing crime.

8. A few years ago the press discovered plans for a new "Office of Strategic Influence"—which when translated means, as best as I could figure it, providing disinformation and lying to outsiders.

9. Obama's February 4, 2009, admission after the Tom Daschle appointment fiasco.

10. Pankaj Mishra, "Rise of the Rest," *London Review of Books*, November 6, 2008; http://www.lrb.co.uk/v30/n21/mish01_.html (accessed March 1, 2008).

11. "Scalia and Torture," in columnist Andrew Sullivan's "The Daily Dish of No Party or Clique," *The Atlantic*, June 19, 2007; http://andrewsullivan.the atlantic.com/the_daily_dish/2007/06/scalia_and_tort.html (accessed March 1, 2009). Another example of digital technology impacting the legal professions is its increasing integration in divorce settlements. Judges are now granting "virtual visitations" with a specified number of online communications via computer per week.

12. The three evening news programs lost 40 percent of their audience between 1981 and 2000. For the first time in any Pew survey, more people say they rely mostly on the Internet for news (40 percent) than cite newspapers (35 percent). With this we have passed another milestone in the informational revolution. The Pew Research Center for the People & the Press, "Internet Overtakes Newspapers as News Outlet," http://peoplepress.orgreport/479/internetovertakesnewspapers asnewssource (accessed March 1, 2009).

13. Writing on his blog for *Atlantic* magazine, Marc Ambinder reports that the National Security Agency has approved a $3,350 smartphone—inevitably dubbed the "BarackBerry"—for Obama's use. The exclusive Sectera Edge, made by General Dynamics, is reportedly capable of encrypting top-secret voice conversations and handling classified documents. See "Obama to Get Spy-Proof Smartphone," http://www.cnn.com/2009/POLITICS/01/22/obama.blackberry/ (accessed March 1, 2009).

14. Evan Ratliff, "Online America," *Wired*, February 2009, 78.

15. The proportion of adult Americans calling themselves Protestants, a steady 63 percent for decades, fell suddenly to 52 percent from 1993 to 2002. In 2004 USAmerica for the first time no longer had a Protestant majority. National Opinion Research Center (NORC), University of Chicago. As reported in David Van Biema, "Roll Over, Martin Luther," *Time*, August 16, 2004, 53. See also "July 20, 2004—America's Protestant Majority Is Fading NORC Research Shows," on the NORC Web site, https://www2.norc.org/about/press 07202004.asp, (accessed March 2, 2009).

16. Callum G. Brown, *The Death of Christian Britain* (London: Routledge, 2001), 1.

17. John Kantor, "A Candidate, His Minister, and the Search for Faith," *New York Times*, April 30, 2007. "The grandparents who helped raise Mr. Obama were nonpracticing Baptists and Methodists. His mother was an anthropologist who collected religious texts the way others picked up tribal masks, teaching her children the inspirational power of the common narratives and heroes." For Obama's own reflections on his religious upbringing, see his *Audacity of Hope* (New York: Crown, 2006), 202–4.

18. Greg Beato, "The Successories President," *Reason*, February 2009, 16; http://www.reason.com/news/show/130841.html (accessed March 2, 2009).

19. President Obama's exact words were, "We are a nation of Christians and Muslims, Jews and Hindus—and non-believers." See "We Will Remake America," 51.

28
HOPE IN 3-D

BRAD R. BRAXTON

During the recent Christmas season, my wife, Lazetta, daughter, Karis, and I spent a wonderful evening with Dr. James and Mrs. Bettye Forbes.[1] They treated us to the Christmas Spectacular at Radio City Music Hall. As we entered the hall, we received some cardboard and plastic 3-D glasses. At a certain point in the show, we put on our 3-D glasses and watched video images of a sleigh ride through New York City on a gigantic movie screen. The 3-D glasses enhanced our viewing experience by adding depth to the images on the screen.

An amazing drama—the election of Barack Obama as president of the United States—has taken place, and it, too, is best viewed with 3-D glasses. As the curtain rises on this new administration, hope is on center stage again after having been upstaged for eight years by presidential recklessness, political deception, and a narrow nationalism. Hope abounds in our country. This is fitting since President Obama identified hope as a central virtue upon which he would hang his presidential administration. As a prelude to his presidential bid, he entitled one of his books *The Audacity of Hope*.

Hope was a crucial aspect of Dr. Martin Luther King's theology. Thus, hope also is a fitting topic for our celebration of the life and legacy of this audacious prophet. Dr. King once wrote, "If you lose hope, somehow you lose that vitality that keeps life moving, you lose that courage to be, that quality that helps you to go on in spite of all."[2] Hope—the quality to go on in spite of all—is on center stage now. Yet even when despair and destruction tried to push hope off the scene, hope continued to hang around, waiting in the wings for decades, even centuries.

Hope elected our first black president in November 2008. *Hope* prompted Jesse Jackson to run for president in 1984 and 1988, therefore making it easier for Barack Obama to run in 2008. *Hope* motivated Barbara Jordan to secure a seat in Congress and become the first African American to deliver a keynote speech at a major party's political convention. Her speech in 1976 made the way for Barack Obama to give his speech at the Democratic National Convention in 2004.

Hope encouraged Shirley Chisholm to run for president, and the 1972 Democratic National Convention was the first major convention in which a woman was considered for president. Shirley Chisholm opened the way for blacks and for women, thus creating the opportunity for both Barack Obama and Hillary Clinton to compete for the presidency.

Hope served as a bulletproof jacket around freedom, even when an assassin's bullet tried to kill freedom's dream at a Memphis motel in 1968. *Hope* kept weary feet marching for voting rights and dignity in the face of vicious dogs and fire hoses. *Hope* resisted the intimidation of those heinous forms of American terrorism known as lynching and slavery. If those trees in Mississippi could talk, and if those plantations in Virginia would divulge their secrets, we would receive testimonies about centuries of terrorism and torture—testimonies reminding us that the United States has been torturing people long before Guantanamo Bay. *Hope* anesthetized black bodies from the suffocating stench on slave ships.

Were it not for hope, this moment in history never would have come. Even when hope was not on center stage in our national discourse, hope has always been present. But this moment in history calls for us to have a deeper understanding of this audacious hope. Given the scope of our problems, a paltry hope, a superficial hope, will not do. We need hope that is not just long and wide. We need hope that is deep and thick. We need hope in three dimensions. It is time now to add depth to our national discussion of hope. We must place spiritual spectacles on our "third eye" so that we apprehend the deeper dimensions of hope. In spiritual matters, it is the third eye that really matters. Regardless of the ability or inability of our physical eyes to provide sight, each of us has a third eye that provides us with moral insight and prophetic foresight. If we peer at hope through spiritual spectacles, we will discover that there are at least three dimensions of hope: an *internal* dimension, an *external* dimension, and an *eternal* dimension. My third eye envisions hope in 3-D.

When I speak of the *internal* dimension of hope, I mean our aspirations for necessary transformations *inside* the Riverside Church. As one of the nation's most prominent religious institutions, we should have hopes for a stronger and better Riverside Church. Our country needs a vibrant, unified Riverside Church.

At the Riverside Church, we have a proud, historic reputation of standing up for peace and justice, but we will place that reputational capital at significant risk if we do not begin to promote peace, justice, patience, and understanding in our own pews. We cannot talk about the injustice of rockets in Gaza if we are launching rhetorical rockets in God's house with mean words and malicious schemes.

In his book *The Audacity of Hope* Barack Obama writes: "What's troubling is the gap between the magnitude of our challenges and the smallness of our politics—the ease with which we are distracted by the petty and trivial, our chronic avoidance of tough decisions, our seeming inability to build a working consensus to tackle any big problem."[3]

If the Riverside Church wants to assist Barack Obama, let us close the gap between our congregation's ideals and our actual congregational practices. We must attend to our internal politics if we are to legitimately offer moral guidance to the body politic.

First, we must abandon a spirit of distrust and fear. Nothing great will happen again at the Riverside Church until we begin placing radical trust in God and in one another in spite of our cultural differences and differences of opinion and approach.

Second, we must stop majoring in minor things. God is saying to this church, "If you will have as much passion for the Bible as you do for church bureaucracy, and if you will live the gospel instead of emotionally maiming each other over minor governance issues, this church will overflow with people and resources to do God's will for this neighborhood and nation."

Third, we must foster a genuine, generous egalitarian pluralism that does not presuppose the unspoken superiority of one culture over another; a pluralism that welcomes a plethora of cultural expressions; a pluralism that generates discomfort, stimulates dialogue, and motivates discipleship.

In addition to the internal hope for the Riverside Church, we also should have *external* hope for our world. By external hope, I mean the aspirations that we have for the world beyond the walls of this church. First, I hope that we will increase, not abandon, our efforts to address the intertwined enemies of racism and poverty. Instead of patting ourselves on the back, let us put our hands to the plow until everyone—regardless of color and economic status—can enjoy the American harvest. A black president is an important milestone on the journey to racial and economic justice, but justice is still being denied to many people of color and to poor people of every race in our country.

The evidence is overwhelming. Brothers still get arrested for DWB (Driving While Brown); less than 1 percent of corporate heads are African Americans; African Americans and Latinos still get "redlined" when trying to secure loans for homes and businesses; and in 2005 the fierce winds of Hurricane Katrina exposed an ironic truth at the heart of the United States' so-called democracy: "colored" people and poor people are more dispensable than white people and wealthy people in this country.

Therefore, I hope that we will use this moment in history to significantly redress the racial and economic injustices that nullify our claims to be a compassionate nation. An advocate for the poor as much as a leader in the civil rights movment, Dr. King said, "True compassion is more than flinging a coin to a beggar; it understands that an edifice which produces beggars needs restructuring."[4]

My second external hope is that we will move beyond any narrow nationalism to a genuine spirit of global interdependence. President Obama, God will judge you and us if we only ask God to bless America, while American policies and practices damn the rest of the world. Perhaps every presidential address should conclude with "God bless *the world*, and let America serve humbly as an agent of that blessing."

Internally we should have hopes for the Riverside Church, and externally we should have hopes for a better world. Finally, we should have an *eternal* hope for the world to come. On this point, the words of Psalm 146:3-5 are poignant: "Do not put your trust in princes, in mortals, in whom there is no help. When their breath departs, they return to the earth; on that very day their plans perish. Happy are those whose help is the God of Jacob, *whose hope is in the LORD their God*" (emphasis added). With all due respect, my eternal hope is not in Barack Obama. I believe God has appointed him to provide leadership in this crucial moment. Yet I urge us to listen to the Bible before we listen to Barack. "Do not put your trust in princes."

Barack Obama is a godly, brilliant, moral man. But in the words of the Bible, he is a prince—a world leader who is constrained like us all by faults, failures, and finitude. Indeed, in the Hebrew of Psalm 146:3-4 there is a play on words. In verse 3, earthly leaders are mortals (Hebrew, *adam*), and in verse 4, they return to the earth (Hebrew, *adamah*).

Let us never forget that Barack Obama is ultimately dust. He is inaugurated dust, but dust nonetheless. As you hear "Hail to the Chief" being played, I also encourage you to hear the play on words in Psalm 146: The president is a mortal (*adam*); and he will return to the ground (*adamah*). My ultimate and eternal hope is not to see this new princely president, but rather to see the Prince of Peace, Jesus Christ.

If you think the crowd that gathered in Washington for Obama's inauguration was something, can you imagine that ultimate,

the audacity of faith

unclouded day when "ten thousand times ten thousand and millions of billions and quadrillions of voices" unite in praise and adoration of our God, who is the only true source of hope?[5] "Happy are those whose help is the God of Jacob, whose hope is in the LORD their God."

I went to Washington for the inauguration of Barack Obama, but my eternal hope is that I will one day have a front row seat at Jesus' coronation. On that day, when we crown Jesus Lord of all, I will shout, "Hallelujah, salvation, and glory!" On that day, we will praise the Lord who will reign—not four years or eight years—but forever, and ever, and ever. Amen.

NOTES

1. James Forbes is senior minister emeritus of the Riverside Church. His wife, Bettye, is the founder and director of the Ebony Ecumenical Ensemble.

2. Martin Luther King Jr., *The Trumpet of Conscience* (New York: Harper & Row, 1968), 76.

3. Barack Obama, *The Audacity of Hope: Thoughts on Reclaiming the American Dream* (New York: Vintage, 2006), 28.

4. Martin Luther King Jr., "Where Do We Go from Here: Chaos or Community?" in *A Testament of Hope: The Essential Writings and Speeches of Martin Luther King, Jr.*, ed. James M. Washington (San Francisco: HarperSanFrancisco, 1986), 630.

5. I am indebted to Washington Monroe Taylor, the father of Gardner C. Taylor, for the phrase "ten thousand times ten thousand and millions of billions and quadrillions of voices." The phrase occurred in "The Eulogy of Reverend E. C. Morris," as delivered by Washington Monroe Taylor, *The African American Pulpit* (Fall 2002): 36.

29
A SENTENCE BEGUN

MELVIN BRAY

It was an election year: a metaphor for moments in which things have stagnated to the point that many are renegotiating political and ideological allegiances. All the usual parties were involved, each of whom had its various strategies for setting the Jewish world right. Ultimately this meant getting rid of the Roman occupiers. The Zealot party was…well…zealous. As usual, they were calling for immediate, decisive action, which if they had their druthers would include slitting some Roman throats and burning a few Roman buildings for good measure. They were convinced that all God was waiting to see was commitment before he would jump in and overturn the Roman oppressor. Meanwhile, the Pharisee party, sympathetic to the Zealots, focused more on the lack of public piety or what some might call "personal responsibility." For them, it was the fault of the drunks, the prostitutes, the gluttons, and those who didn't pay their tithes to the temple that God hadn't begun to champion the Jewish cause.

On the other hand, the Herodians and Sadducees were the political pragmatists of their day. They saw "the Zealots and Pharisees as hopelessly naive: nobody could defeat the Romans militarily, and to try would be suicide. So, following the old wisdom of 'If you can't beat them, join them,' or 'If you can't beat them, at least try to make a profit off of them,' they called for a path of accommodation and coexistence." As far as they were concerned, they couldn't be accused of collusion. "'It was just being realistic,' a Jewish tax collector might say, to the chagrin of those Jews who couldn't so easily nestle up to the powers that be." Then there were

the audacity of faith

a few like the Essenes who rejected all of these approaches, calling instead for a withdrawal into the wilderness to try to avoid the whole simmering mess. Jesus didn't fit neatly into any of these camps. His was a postpartisan campaign. He had no institutional backing, just a few generous patrons and populous support. [1]

It had been a long, hard-fought competition for the hearts and minds of the Palestinian people. Jesus' opponents had dogged his steps for nearly three years, trying to discredit him in the eyes of the public. There was something about the status quo they desperately wanted to maintain. Yet his message had won increasing support. "A new administration is as close as your willingness to participate in it," he would say. It was a message so full of hope that some like Nicodemus and Zacchaeus, who had voted Pharisee and Sadducee all their lives, defected to Jesus' cause.

It is easy to think poorly of these religious leaders, who were also the local political leaders, of Jesus' day. However, it could not have been any easier for them than it was for us to watch candidate Obama thumb his nose at the political establishment by in essence saying, "Both liberals and conservatives have been squabbling over campaign finance reform for thirty years and big-money interest peddling has only gotten worst. So I'm going to subvert the system as it exists and show up both sides by raising the most money ever in a presidential campaign, only with an average contribution amount of less than a hundred bucks!"[2] Many didn't know how to react. Should we be upset at him for changing the rules without asking permission? Or should we thank God that someone did?

Jesus must have had some sense of the ideological difficulties his campaign was causing, because in that moment he chose to enact an object lesson to serve as an interpretive lens for his supporters. At least that is how the authors Matthew and Mark recount the story. On the way into Jerusalem one morning, Jesus came across a fig tree that was lush with big, beautiful, out-turned leaves. Now, anyone from that part of the world during that time understood that a fig tree only began to present its leaves when its fruit was ripe for the picking. To Jesus' dismay, the gorgeous green tree was empty—not one fig to be found. And in response to its uselessness—in what appeared to be a startling loss of campaign discipline—Jesus pronounced the shortest blessing over a meal, or lack thereof, in his life. "God, damn it!" he said in effect with disgust.

He continued on into the city and into the temple where, in ironic repetition of his uncommon display of vehemence along the way, he gave the media even more red meat by overturning tables and causing a virtual riot. The irony is his stated rationale: his protest was over something that had been denied someone else. Is that even possible? Shouldn't he be worried about securing his own place at the table first? He who had himself been denied; he who had been reviled. Why, it seems like just the day before, at the big march on Jerusalem, the people were all but ready to crown him king. This was his time to shine, his moment in the sun.

Instead, his interest was in peasants being cheated by the money-changers as they converted the peasants' Roman coins (which were not permitted in the temple) into proper Jewish currency (which was permitted because it did not bear the image of Caesar). Jesus was repulsed by merchants who baited two days wages out of subsistence farmers for a pair of spotless turtledoves that were then switched, while the buyer wasn't looking, for blemished birds. Jesus couldn't abide priests denying those same farmer peasants God's forgiveness because they were found guilty of bringing blemished sacrifices to the Lord, which meant the farmers had to pay a penalty of forty days' wages in order to come again before the Lord. Jesus knew the priests were not only the adjudicators of debt to God but also of debts owed to the wealthy landowners on whose land these sharecroppers would have to farm even longer in order to pay off their temple debts. Thus he recognized that many acts of forgiveness denied were simply the attempts of crooked priests to enrich themselves through kickbacks from money-changers, merchants, and wealthy landowners for a scam well run. Solomon's temple had become an insiders' game that was crushing the life out of the common people. And instead of demanding his own seat on the gravy train, Jesus demanded that the temple become a house of provision "for all people."

The telling of this story has implicated me in many ways over the years. What strikes me at this moment is that the quintessential ideology of all Jesus' political opponents is only self-interest. By modern standards there is little wrong with this. They are merely seeking the best they can imagine for themselves and others like themselves. However, what was proposed in word and deed by Jesus, the candidate who had captured the imaginations of the people, was *others' interests*. Even after Jesus cursed the fig tree in association with the religious leaders for being uselessly self-involved, he turned around and told his disciples that real power lies not in the ability to denounce, but in their ability to give and forgive (and thereby redeem). Even in the face of legitimate personal grievance—when the natural inclination is to seek retribution—in Mark's telling of this story (11:12-26), the implication of Jesus' words and actions are profoundly unambiguous: seek the good of others.

This kind of thinking is radical—revolutionary—the kind of thinking that turns conventional wisdom on its head. I would to God that we Americans could see ourselves in this story. Not because the circumstances are identical or even substantively similar, but because that is what good stories allow us to do—to see ourselves, our better selves.

At the beginning of this new chapter in the American story, I wish that all those who feel they won with the election of President Barack Hussein Obama could resist the desire to settle old scores. I would that we could see that the possibilities created by forgiveness are far more compelling than those predicated on exacting a pound of flesh from one's opponents. Whether with health-care reform or with the desire to investigate the Bush administration for war crimes, I pray we live out of the same graciousness that newly elected President Obama showed when he appointed Hillary Clinton secretary of state. I pray we come to understand why Obama immediately enacted stimulus measures that included conservative ideas, though conservatives themselves snubbed him. I pray we simply forgive.

Also, I pray that African Americans in particular, who take such legitimate pride in President Obama's rise to prominence, would embrace the causes of others as our own, so much so that we demand that our gains be gains for all people. We are off to an uneven start. Many of us have been so intent on rectifying our own disenfranchisement that we have neglected the enfranchisement of others. In our churches we offer excuses or what we believe to be biblical rationale for our hypocritical biases against gender, sexual orientation, disability, religion, or national origin, ignoring that much of the same reasoning made us second-class citizens for hundreds of years. We quietly sulk about how annoying it is to have immigrants use their native languages around those of us who only speak English and want to demand that when "they" come to "our country," "they" should at least have to learn English. We bemoan the financial and practical inconvenience of having to make programs and facilities handicap accessible, or we flat out ignore all together the responsibility to do so. Additionally, we establish unspoken rules of functioning that preclude women from certain jobs or penalize them when they execute a job differently than their male counterparts. Furthermore, we deem it acceptable when authorities profile as potential threats any person who shows religious devotion by covering his or her head in public. And we seek to legislate against the equal enfranchisement of fellow citizens simply because they want to claim someone of the same sex as spouse in wills and on insurance forms.

Those inspired by the others-interested ethic of the Jesus way must embrace historically marginalized people not as just "the least of these" (a nifty yet objectifying slogan), but complete the thought and see them as "the least of these [our] brothers [and sisters]." We must realize that disenfranchisement anywhere is a threat to enfranchisement everywhere. We must make room for all. We must, in a word, give.

Give. Forgive. Seek the good of others. Such simple words. So full of redemption. But they have absolutely no legitimacy if those of us who claim to follow in the way of Jesus don't see them as realistic political alternatives. Perhaps we shy away from such ideas, such words, because we know what they cost Jesus and we fear the same for ourselves.

the audacity of faith

As we begin this next brave chapter in the American story, it is our choice—as individuals—what ideas and what words will define us. "In today's sharp sparkle, this winter air, anything can be made, any sentence begun."³ What will the words of that sentence be?

NOTES

1. This description of each of the political parties of Jesus' day is quoted and paraphrased from chapter 10 of Brian D. McLaren, *Everything Must Change: Jesus, Global Crises, and a Revolution* (Nashville: Thomas Nelson, 2007).

2. Of course it depends on how one does the math, but top estimates put the average donation amount at no more than $250 per contributor—with only 20-something percent coming from persons who donated the maximum $2,300 for either or both the primary and the general election.

3. Elizabeth Alexander, "Praise Song for the Day," inaugural poem delivered at President Barack Obama's inauguration, January 20, 2009.

30

WHAT MEAN THESE STONES?
The Election of Barack Obama in Retrospect and Prospect

HAROLD DEAN TRULEAR

I watched her run circles around the gym, seemingly oblivious to the history in which her mother involved her. Her African braids flowed in the musty air lingering from countless middle school physical education classes. Her arms stretched wide as if she understood what it meant to soar—soar as the man whom five hundred people stood in queue to support on a dismal day in a black working-class suburb of Philadelphia. She could not have been more than five years old. Could she appreciate her place in the surrounding exuberance? Would her mother, who carefully watched her circular flight plan across the gym floor, tell her one day, "What mean these stones?" (see Joshua 4:6).

Only the weather was dismal. The mood was jubilant, fervent, and literally transcendent. Black people stood in line without complaint and with hope. "Victory is mine!" shouted a local pastor upon her exit from the dusky gym. I saw poll workers with business casual and poll workers with backward baseball caps. Seniors on canes and "boyz" in the hood stood together, and no one nervously clutched her purse. It was history. But what mean these stones?

I have never been prouder to be a black man. Proud because I felt part of something—a community that did not care that I am a card-carrying Republican. Proud because they knew how I would vote. I would vote for the men and women who gave their lives that this day might come to pass. So when I voted for Barack Obama, I dug deep with no regrets. It was a vote for him—and for Viola Liuzzo, Michael Schwerner, Andrew Goodman, James Chaney, and Rev. James Reeb. Medgar Evers and Emmett Till, being dead, yet speaketh. They are stones.

If those names are less familiar to you than those of weak presidents, such as Buchanan, Grant, and Pierce, then you get my point. The platform of the presidency has elevated men unworthy of the office. Whether Obama will become as those weak leaders or history will proclaim him to rank with Lincoln and Roosevelt will be determined by time. Indeed, the stones gain meaning not from their erection in the Jordan, but from the meaningful nature of the subsequent conquest of Canaan. The hope engendered by Obama's candidacy transcends the power of his message. African Americans stood in long lines, in a misty rain, and in full view of racist antagonists to say, "This is one of us," despite the fact that his father was an African and his mother was white. The accident of history identifying any person of color as a Negro enables blacks with a long history of dealing with racism to identify with a man who does not share all of their history, but by color and commitment lays claim to their predicament.

So I joined the party of the people of the predicament—the girl with the braids, the seniors on canes, the families voting together, the cars driving by honking their support, and the revivalist fervor of a people who felt that this time they had a voice. It was the voice of those who stood—no, marched—for the rights of those who now stood for hours to vote. The voice cried, "My feet are tired but my soul is rested." How dare anyone complain about the blood rushing to feet standing in the voting line when compared to the blood shed for a democracy celebrated across the planet? Blood flowed and feet blistered that the orator—he of the preacher's rhythmic call and response ("Yes, we can")—would be the next president of the United States. Change and hope kissed on an autumn night celebrating a union that felt religious—transcendent, almost otherworldly—in a world of pragmatic politics specializing in the art of the possible.

Transcendent—that's spiritual stuff. A spirit of American and even African American revivalism grew in the days approaching the election. Many congregations and religious bodies organized prayer vigils on both sides of the partisan sea. As in 2004, one group emerged convinced that their prayers were answered. Those who believed that they would never see an African American president in their lifetime attributed Barack Obama's victory to divine intervention. Organizations prayed for candidates committed to issues as varied as assistance for the poor, the sanctity of one man–one woman marriage, and even the counting of votes. Prayers lifted from the lips of Protestants, the pens of Catholic bishops, and the wisdom of Jewish rabbis.

While praying for a campaign does not constitute new behavior, the more public display of faith on the Democratic side had not been seen since the civil rights movement (when there was a somewhat different Democratic Party). Indeed, African American communities recalled images of the religious fervor of the civil rights movement in the grassroots similarities between the marches of the sixties and the Obama campaign organization of 2007–2008. Obama's own acceptance speech both borrowed from ("We as a people will get there") and referenced the work of Martin Luther King, as did several pundits and newscasts. One TV broadcast even juxtaposed King's "I have a dream" speech with Obama' election night address.

Such comparisons give insight to the meaning of the stones. The reality is that this election cannot be understood apart from history, nor can it be interpreted without due consideration of the activity of God. Just as King declared that the "arc of the moral universe is long but it bends toward justice," Obama's election reflected a place on that trajectory painted by a divine hand within the shadows "behind the dim unknown…keeping watch above his own." The stones say, "God has done this." Yet biblical history is clear that one can never remain stuck on the stones any more than Jesus could grant Peter's request to build three tabernacles on the Mount of Transfiguration.

Subsequent to the placing of the stones in the Jordan, the children of Israel faced the great task of possessing Canaan. Before them lay a painful consecration, a series of dusty marches, the challenges of audacious faith, and a personal conversation between their new leader and a Sage Adviser who transcended partisan politics, declaring, "I didn't come to take sides, I came to take over!"

The stones could not be fully invested with meaning, however, until after Canaan's conquest. Similarly, the meaning of Barack Obama's election cannot be fully grasped until a similar occupation. An economic downturn turned up, a war on terror reframed, the unfinished business of education and health care for the dispossessed addressed, the reform of the criminal justice system accelerated. Giants roam Canaan, and their conquest fully defines the stones.

African Americans will need to be patient and participatory, prayerful and prophetic. Patience comes when one understands that presidents are not kings and must practice a brand of statecraft that includes negotiation, compromise, persuasion, and vision. The president's promise of bipartisan leadership is a noble sentiment, yet every president since George Washington has tripped over the stumbling blocks of opposing parties. Transcending partisan politics, especially in a nation that has only one party more than did the former Soviet Union, requires nothing less miraculous than the Captain's takeover. The presidency is limited by checks and balances that hamper any individual's ability to lead, no matter how visionary that leader might be.

Christian citizenship requires participation. While Martin Luther King Jr. was clearly a leader, his genius also lay in the recognition that he must have followers. Obama's community organizing skills show that he understands the power of participation. African Americans must now resist the "spectator spirit" and become involved in lobbying, organizing, and agitating at the community, municipal, county, and state levels in order for meaningful change to come from this presidential administration. Vision may come from the top down, but change comes from the bottom up. Grassroots movements rock the world, from the dingy manger in Bethlehem, to the hard streets of Chicago, to the dusty roads of

Alabama. Failure to act on local issues close to home for African Americans, such as quality schools, health care, crime and criminal justice reform, and so on, will further paralyze any national vision for change.

The African American church must also pray, not only because of the mandate given in Romans 13 to pray for those in authority, but also because of its promise that government's ordination is by God and for good. God desires to use this and all administrations for the advancement of good and for the restraint of evil. Given the preponderance of self-interest, greed, and suffering in our nation and world, it only makes sense to assault the battlements of glory for effective warfare against principalities and powers that threaten life on earth. To pray for President Obama (and not just that he will not be assassinated) is an audacious act of faith declaring that no matter how excited we are about his election, there is more work to be done, and he will need what Nehemiah acknowledged when he said, "The gracious hand of my God was upon me" (Nehemiah 2:8).

We cannot overlook the notion that African Americans may have to speak a word of prophetic challenge to this president. Forgotten in the public media lynching of the prophet Jeremiah (Wright) was his clear statement that once Barack Obama was elected, "I'm coming after him, too." African Americans must always hold even their most beloved political leaders accountable. The Hebrew prophets spoke to "their own" when they addressed the kings of Israel and Judah, and used the first person plural to reflect on the objects of prophetic utterance. Therefore, where there is disagreement in the African American community with the policies and performance of this president, the example of the prophets of the Old Testament mandate that we be prophetic as well. President Obama's human dignity requires he be held accountable, as should be the case for anyone in authority. While some have bemoaned the development of the black church as a "non-prophet organization" in the eight years under Bush-Cheney, one can actually trace the roots of the decline of prophetic presence to the earliest days of the post–civil rights era.

What mean these stones? We will fully know when the little girl running circles through the gym matures. For now we content ourselves with the image of her soaring with an energy reminding us of the highest aspirations of the human spirit. Her presence in an intergenerational gathering of voters who did not complain about the two- and three-hour wait at the polls reminds us of the lines of marchers who put their lives on the line so that we might stand in this new line. No one was tired. There was a borrowed strength from feet that had marched and the knees that had been bent in prayer. It was the spirit of revival.

31
THE OBAMA PRESIDENCY AND AMERICA'S UNFINISHED BUSINESS

OTIS MOSS JR.

The Declaration of Independence was a charter for a new nation. Abraham Lincoln said it was "a new nation conceived in liberty and dedicated to the proposition that all men are created equal." But Jefferson's "charter" did not end slavery. It did not end gender discrimination, Native American genocide, anti-Catholicism, or anti-Semitism. Thomas Jefferson's Declaration did not free Jefferson's slaves or his black mistress. It did not free the slaves of George Washington nor of Patrick Henry who declared, "Give me liberty or give me death." I have often wondered what would have happened in Patrick Henry's house when he uttered those famous words if all his slaves had stood up and declared, "We agree, and we demand the same!"

At the end of the Revolutionary War for Independence, America was left with unfinished business. Business that had to be taken up by Richard Allen, Frederick Douglass, Harriet Tubman, Sojourner Truth, Abraham Lincoln, Harriet Beecher Stowe, Thaddeus Stevens, Charles Sumner, Generals Grant and Sherman, and many more.

The Civil War and the abolitionist movement gave us the Thirteenth, Fourteenth, and Fifteenth Amendments to the U.S. Constitution. These put an end to legalized slavery and offered citizenship and voting rights to former slaves, but they did not prevent another hundred years of lynching, apartheid, and Ku Klux Klan violence.

The Civil War of the 1860s saved the Union, which was Lincoln's passion. The war abolished slavery, which was a moral and political necessity, but the unfinished business of Reconstruction was the urgency of the civil rights movement—an urgency that faces us today in glaring poverty and racial and gender disparities, and in the words of Jonathan Kozol, "savage inequalities" in education.

January 20, 2009, was an unprecedented moment of celebration and achievement. But there stands before us decades of continuing struggles. There stands before us a set of profound realities. We are called to be the "trumpet of conscience" in an age of agony and change.

Let it never be forgotten that the charter for a new nation did not end slavery. The abolitionist movement ended slavery but not the rule of racism and sexism.

The appointment of two African American surgeon generals did not close the health disparity gaps or end the spread of HIV/AIDS. The appointment of a black secretary of health and human services and secretary of housing and urban development did not remove the disparity in health and housing and the need for a humane urban policy. The appointment of two African American secretaries of state did not remove the need for a yet-to-be-born, comprehensive and coherent African policy. It did not stop postcolonial massacres or the slaughter in Darfur.

The 1954 Supreme Court Decision was "a joyous daybreak after a long and desolate midnight," said Martin Luther King Jr., but it did not prevent the abandonment of public education. In a most paradoxical way, *Brown v. Board of Education* (1954) intensified all the reactionary and demonic forces. That outcome of that case was as necessary as sunlight and raindrops. But the forces of darkness and the famine of futility still stalked the American landscape.

Old agonies die slowly, but they do eventually die. Unfortunately, however, new demons tend to succeed them. The Emancipation Proclamation was an act long before it was a fact.

What, then, does the election of President Barack Obama mean to America and the world? First, it breaks the shackles of racial dogma and sets forth a new and creative energy in our nation.

More than two hundred years ago, the U.S. Constitution defined black people as three-fifths of a person. In those days, neither a black man nor a white woman was allowed to vote. The journey from three-fifths of a person to the Oval Office is a remarkable journey: "We have come over a way that with tears has been watered. We have come, treading our path through blood of the slaughtered."

The Obama election is a new star in the sky of little children. Talking with a group of children following the election, I asked, "What does Obama's election mean to you?" With great elation and in unison, they shouted, "Yes, we can!" It will be ten years or more before they can vote, but they are already enfranchised in a thousand ways that Washington, Jefferson, Madison, and Monroe never dreamed of. The ballot must be in the hearts of our children years before it is in their hands.

Dr. King often talked about black people in the South who did not vote because they could not vote and black people in the North who did not vote because they believed they had nothing for which to vote. Today those shackles have been broken. However, we must "keep our eyes on the prize," because old agonies die slowly and new demons are born in every generation.

There are those among us even now who would repeal the Voting Rights Bill based on the false notion that it is no longer needed. We must never forget the tragedies of post-Reconstruction. From 1876 to 1896, a short period of twenty years, a new era of racism was legalized, codified, and institutionalized. Thus the election of President Obama calls for creative realists.

In 1960 I listened to Dr. King give a profound analysis of the struggle for racial justice. In his message he talked about the twin dangers of extreme optimism and extreme pessimism. The misguided optimist takes the position that progress rolls in on the wheels of inevitability; therefore we can just be patient and everything will be all right. The pessimist takes the position that the dream is futile, the task is in vain, nothing good is about to happen. Both the extreme optimist and the pessimist tend to agree on one thing: we should sit down and do nothing. But the creative

the audacity of faith

realist takes the position that the struggle is long, the road is rough, and the hill is high, but if we are willing to serve and suffer, dream and labor, we can create a new era. It is important that we see the election of Barack Obama, not through the eyes of extreme optimism or the defeatism of pessimistic inertia, but rather through the eyes of creative realism.

President Obama has inherited an unfinished agenda. Democracy is an unfinished cathedral. Each generation must make an intentional contribution toward a "more perfect union." We must not sit around and wait for President Obama to complete what Presidents Lincoln, Roosevelt, Truman, Kennedy, Johnson, Carter, and Clinton were not able to complete. We must do our part during this momentous period to help President Obama and the nation cross turbulent streams and climb the rough side of the mountain. Out of the Christian tradition, we know that resurrection is not the end but a new beginning.

We saw this after the victories of World War II when we had the difficult task of rebuilding Japan and Europe. We also had the urgent task of retooling our own nation and providing education, health, housing, and jobs for the veterans and their families. But with this tremendous investment in the future, America became a stronger and greater nation.

This is not a postracial era. It is a gigantic breakthrough and the injection of a special transfusion of hope into the veins and arteries of our common life. This is one of America's great opportunities to write an enduring chapter of greatness in our nation's history. What we do with this moment will determine the kind of nation our children and our children's children will inherit.

Out of the Jewish tradition we can say, "The time is short, the hour is late, the business is urgent. It is not incumbent upon us to finish the task; neither are we free to desist from doing all we can." And the poet Louis Untermeyer prayed, "Even when the fight is won, God keep me still unsatisfied."

The Obama presidency is a call to each of us to work even harder while we celebrate. It is a challenge to America not to let this harvest pass. The election of President Obama is an answered prayer.

Now we must deal faithfully and courageously with the challenge of answered prayers. We hold in our hands a great trophy, but we must not set it on the shelf of historic memory. We must pass it on as a runner in a great relay. If we stand still, we not only lose the race, but abuse the blessing of participation.

We are surrounded by a great cloud of witnesses who died on the battlefields of history and hope. They turned haunting fears into hymns of faith. They built bridges over troubled waters. They spent time behind bars. They slept on cold steel and cement. They felt the hangman's rope around their necks. But they would not give up.

We have more rivers to cross and more mountains to climb, but we have a president to whom God has given mountain-moving faith, mountain-climbing strength, and mountain-claiming wisdom.

Let us labor together on this unfinished cathedral of democracy. Let us preach, teach, and practice the unconditional love of Jesus Christ. Let us turn this great moment into a great century of love, justice, truth, reconciliation, and peace.

To God be the glory!

32

WHERE DO WE GO FROM HERE?

OTIS MOSS III

Where do we go from here? In the words of James Weldon Johnson, "We have come, treading our path through the blood of the slaughtered. Out of the gloomy past, till now we stand at last to where the white gleam of our bright star is cast." Did we ever think we would live to see such a day? An African American is now serving as the president of the United States of America! People have been celebrating all across the country.

I have really enjoyed the celebrations I've seen across the globe. I've seen people in Osaka, Japan, shouting up a storm. I've seen the Aborigines in Australia shouting and dancing. The Mowry people in New Zealand were shouting and dancing. Those in South Africa were doing the "toi toi." Dancing broke out in every village and hamlet in Kenya. Even in Palestine and Israel people laid claim to this moment. In France they are speaking in a completely different way about the new possibilities for America.

My wife, Monica, and I are not yet able to completely grasp what has happened. When we went to vote on Election Day, we stood next to a girl no more than fourteen who began to cry. By the time she is finally able to cast her first vote at eighteen, the idea of having an African American president will be normal for her.

I was disturbed, however, by the pundits who announced that the struggle against racism is now over. As I began to pray and reflect with reference to this moment, I found in the first chapter of the book of Joshua some insight as to where we go from here.

The text is about an earth-shattering, history-making moment of transition. In the book of Joshua, God's people had to be realigned, readjusted, and reoriented to live in a post-wilderness time and a pre–Promised Land phase. It is a post-Moses moment as Joshua ascends to the leadership of the people, and it quickly becomes clear that things are going to be just a little different. The old landmarks can no longer be used. There will be no more manna from heaven and no more water from rocks.

Let me update this scene. There will be no more living in shotgun houses and no more picking cotton in the wilderness. Things are going to be a little different. As it was for Israel, slavery is a part of our history, and there are those who are making the claim that we have reached the Promised Land. A generation has arisen standing a few miles away from the land flowing with milk and honey. This new generation has no memory of the segregated days back in Egypt. They will live the majority of their lives in a free society.

These people with their stories of wilderness oppression and segregation are an aging population who will soon be off the scene. This next generation is on the edge of the Promised Land and is poised to live a life of which their ancestors could only dream. They must beware, however, because the most dangerous time is when you are just out of the wilderness but have not yet crossed into the Promised Land. Sometimes we confuse our promised moment with the Promised Land.

Things have changed. Moses is now gone from the scene. The progenitor of theology and the professor of pastoral care is dead. The people celebrate his sacrifice once a year with a Moses holiday on which children recite the "Let my people go" sermon. They give only a snippet of the speech, never the whole; otherwise they would have to talk about the plagues, the blood, and the pain they had to go through to reach this post-wilderness moment. They love talking about that grand nonviolent march on the mall near the Red Sea as people gathered to move from one point to another.

Now Joshua has moved to this moment when he is elected leader of this yet-to-be nation. It is a nation with great economic hardship. No one even thought that a man so young could ascend to the highest office of the land. The last time this happened in the history of the Hebrew people was during the Hebrew reconstruction period when Joseph came out of slavery and was elevated to second in command next to Pharaoh. Moses is now dead. Joshua has taken the reins of leadership, and all seems to be right with the world. There will be no more oppression, no more class-based imperialism, and no manifest destiny perpetrated against indigenous people. We now can get beyond the horrific moment of history called slavery, because some are saying all is right in the world.

But please hold on before we go any further with this analysis. Many who watched the rise of Joshua want to declare that all social actions, political critiques, and protest efforts are outdated, irrelevant, and unnecessary. It is true that Joshua and his people are free. It is true that there is no more slavery. It is true that there is no more legally segregated housing. It is true that domestic terrorists wearing white sheets no longer haunt the wilderness of the southern border of Egypt. It is true that there is no more lynching for the sons and daughters of Egypt. It seems they have come a mighty long way. They are living in a post-wilderness time and a pre-promise moment. They made it through the wilderness, and they can see the Promised Land. There are many wonderful, new possibilities.

Nevertheless, the people are actually between the perils of yesterday and the promises of tomorrow. If this text has anything to tell us today, it is this: we, too, are in the midst of a promised moment, but we must not confuse that with the Promised Land. God has done amazing things, but there is still work to do. Joshua has the resources and the wherewithal to cross the Jordan for himself. He has the physical stamina to move himself into the land of milk and honey. But liberation is not achieved when one leader can cross into the Promised Land. Joshua's success is defined not by individual success, but by collective progress. He never gets excited by the fact that he can cross into the Promised Land alone. His definition of success is if the entire nation can make it into the Promised Land.

The same is true for us today. I would submit to you that the election of Barack Obama is without a doubt one of the greatest moments in American history. Nevertheless, we must be sure that our shouts of triumph are peppered with the sobering reality that our broader struggle for human dignity is not yet over. From this moment on, we as a nation and we as a people must work to make this moment in time not merely a cosmic coincidence but a historical trend. We still have work to do, and I believe that Joshua has some lessons for us as we face a post-wilderness moment though are not yet in the Promised Land.

Notice in this text that while you are living in a Joshua moment, you can never forget the Moses generation. This moment did not fall out of the sky. A history surrounds this moment. A Moses generation sits in the balcony of heaven looking down on these events. It is because of the sacrifices of Moses that Joshua is even possible. Our history is full of people who are our Moseses, both named and unnamed: Harriet Tubman, Nat Turner, Frederick Douglass, Marian Wright Stewart, Booker T. Washington, Ida B. Wells, W. E. B. DuBois, Marcus Garvey—the list goes on—A. Phillip Randolph, Claude McKay, Alain Locke, Ella Baker, Diane Nash, James Nash, Malcolm X, Martin Luther King Jr.…

We must never think we got to this moment by ourselves. It is because of the Moses generation that we have come to this moment in history. To those in the Joshua generation, I say, never think so highly of yourself that you believe your own hype as if you pulled yourself up by your bootstraps. There was a moment in time when you didn't have boots. You didn't even have flip-flops. You didn't have anything. It was a generation now long gone that prepared the country for this moment. Joshua understands, as the text says, "As I was with Moses, so I will be with you." In other words, you must know that your rise to power is directly related to the Moses generation. You will be the one who will have to take the people into the Promised Land, but never forget there was a generation who lived in the wilderness working and praying for this day.

There is a second thing this text teaches us as we face this moment in history. The text says that "every place you put your foot will be yours." In other words, "Wherever you walk, even though you have never been in that space before, you must be able to lay claim to what I have already promised you."

Several years ago there was an elderly woman who just started walking outside the White House. Everywhere she put her foot, she

the audacity of faith

laid claim to the space. She did not live to see this moment, but I believe she understood something that our Native American brothers and sisters understand. They have a ritual called "the rain dance." They never dance after the rain begins to fall; they always begin their dance before the rain appears. Everywhere they put their foot, they are saying that God is going to water that spot. What we must begin to understand as a people is that God has already prepared some things for us, but we must walk and act as if that is so.

Of course, we must understand that even when we move into the Promised Land, there is still work to do. We still have children with no fathers at home. Our work is not done. Our high school drop out rate is 50 percent. Our work is not done. HIV is on the rise in our community. Our work is not done. Forty-five million people in this country are without health care. Our work is not done. Our children operate within a culture of disrespect. Our work is not done.

We cannot be satisfied with the status quo. Let us not be satisfied with the way the world is right now. Let us not be satisfied "until justice rolls down like water and righteousness like a mighty stream." Let us not be satisfied until every child is pulled out of poverty. Let us not be satisfied until black males no longer make up the majority in our state and federal prison facilities. Let us not be satisfied until brothers pull up their pants and until some sisters close their legs. Let us not be satisfied until we have reached where God has called us to reach.

If God can take a young man who was sitting in this pew, heard a preacher preach from this pulpit, and was stirred in his soul to the point that it set his feet on a path to the presidency, then we cannot know what else God is going to do. Maybe there is another president sitting here. Maybe another generation is being birthed who is going to do great things. I don't know what God will do, but I know that God is still in the blessing business.

We must work on, we must march on, we must sing on, we must praise on, we must pray on. God has called us to a mighty walk. We are not done. Where do we go from here? We must have the audacity to move beyond this promise moment and finally possess the Promised Land.

33
FOR SUCH A TIME AS THIS[1]

DERRICK HARKINS

The story of Esther is a gripping drama. We look on as the very survival of a people hangs in the balance. Of course, the truth that is so clearly visible is that deliverance and salvation can make their way through even in the worst of circumstances. Isn't it good to know that when evil and pain are surrounding us and would seem to overtake us, we still have a claim on being able to overcome? Mordecai says it clearly: relief and deliverance will come.

As we read this story, we will not only encounter certain truths that Mordecai was determined to communicate to Esther, but we will encounter some important truths for our own lives as well.

Here is the first truth to be shared from the story of Esther: *God prepares us for God's purposes.* What a wondrous thing to look over our shoulder and see the moments and circumstances that we may not have understood or may have discounted as unimportant. Even those things that frustrated us or were painful have been part of our shaping and molding. Perhaps, as Mordecai would say, those challenges and hardships occurred "for such a time as this." When I am groping through the valleys of my life, it surely helps to remember that "all things work together for good for those who love God, who are called according to his purpose" (Romans 8:28).

The book of Esther reminds us that God's preparation can often be confounding. Consider Martin Luther King Jr. who was born into the privilege of a prominent black middle-class pastor's family. This young intellectual was capable enough to enter Morehouse College at the age of fifteen, and he was determined enough to earn a Ph.D. in systematic theology from Boston University at the age of

the audacity of faith

twenty-six. How could it be that he was being prepared to do anything but have a long and productive career in the genteel world of academia? Consider Dietrich Bonheoffer, a celebrated Lutheran pastor and theologian from Germany who was as enlightened by his time in Harlem and at the Abyssinian Baptist Church of New York City as he was by his time at Union Theological Seminary in that same city. How could it be that he was being prepared to do anything but find refuge during the war and write and teach far removed from Hitler's terror?

How could it be that Rosa Parks would lead anything but a life of normalcy as a housekeeper and seamstress in Montgomery, Alabama? How could it be that the first black president of the *Harvard Law Review* would do anything but dwell at the lofty heights of the best corporate law firms in the country? How could it be? Surely that is what he was being prepared to do!

Like Esther, we may begin with the desire to stay where things are predictable and comfortable. But thank God for the Mordecais in our lives. Thank God for the voices of those persons who stir our spirits to move beyond what is safe and secure and then prod us to proceed to do what is right and just and necessary. Mordecai posed a provocative and, maybe for some of us, disturbing proposition. "Who knows? Perhaps you are where you are for such a time as this." You see, while the gospel should comfort us, it also should compel us. In coming to worship, one should hear sermons that soothe the spirit; but one should also hear a word from the Lord that can disquiet the heart. We ought not to rest easy until we are caught up in what God has called us to do.

How could it be that a young man like Bonhoeffer, thirty-nine at the time of his death at the hand of the Nazis, could understand that God had beckoned him far away from what was predictable and easy? How could it be that any of us are prodded and prompted by the testimonies of the Mordecais in our lives? Maybe, like Fannie Lou Hamer, it means we become "sick and tired of being sick and tired."

Here is the second point to be garnered from this story about Mordecai and Esther: *the God who prepares us then proceeds to place us where we are most needed.* Bonhoeffer would not remain in the safe refuge of writing and teaching, for God had prepared him and then placed him to serve as a voice for brave discipleship in the face of Nazi oppression. Rosa Parks would not have just another normal bus ride home at the end of another long day on the job. Instead, God prepared her and then placed her at the center of a long journey that would break down barriers of segregation. Martin King would not, as the hymnist might say, live "on flowery beds of ease" in the ivory tower of academia. Instead, God prepared him and then placed him to be "a drum major for justice."

At the beginning of this year, none of us knew who Chesley Sullenberger was. This fifty-seven-year-old man had been an airline pilot for thirty years. Could it be that all those years of routine flights and those thousands of hours in the air were preparation for him to be placed where he was so he could do what he did within just seven minutes? Seven minutes—that is how long it took for him to turn death and disaster into a miraculous airplane landing in the middle of the Hudson River. As in the book of Esther, where the word *God* never actually appears, no one on that airplane may have seen God's hand at the outset. But I am persuaded that somewhere between nine hundred feet in the air and the surface of the water, God showed up in a wonderful and powerful way. Oh yes, first God prepares us; then God places us in situations of great challenge and sometimes danger where we can do what God has called us to do at any given moment in history.

Now, Mr. Obama, while I am tasked with preaching to everyone who is here today, let me step aside to speak with you for just a moment. In doing so, let me borrow Mordecai's conjecture. Perhaps, just perhaps, you are where you are, for such a time as this. Oh, yes, it is fair to say that the votes of the people are what placed you in the office to which you were elected, but it will be God's strength that sustains you.

Perhaps your entire family has been shaped and fashioned for such a time as this. Here you sit—a mother, a father, and two daughters who have been prepared with depth of character and spiritual strength, so that even if the bright light of acclaim should

the audacity of faith

sometime shift to the harsh glare of criticism, you will know the foundation upon which you stand. If you, Mr. and Mrs. Obama, and all of us as well, can consider that God has a purpose and place for each one of us, we can be like this brave woman of Scripture and go forward in prayerfulness and faithfulness.

Esther realized that she could not keep silent. Do you know what I think Esther was saying? Pardon my exegetical liberties here, but I think she was saying, "There is a fire shut up in my bones, and I cannot keep it to myself." I think Esther was saying that the unseen hand of an amazing God was leading, guiding, and directing her life.

Perhaps we can do as Esther did. She told Mordecai to fast even as she would do with her maidens. It is not presumptuous to understand that along with fasting came prayer. And likewise, we can assume to know that Esther reached deep into the reservoir of God's faithful strength as she began her task. She then famously said, "I will go to see the king; and if I perish, I perish." She was not saying that she had a wish for martyrdom. No, she was saying boldly that she would trust God no matter the circumstance.

Once more, in that same sense of commitment, Dietrich Bonhoeffer said, "Action springs not from thought, but from a readiness for responsibility." Fannie Lou Hamer said, "Sometimes it seems that to tell the truth today is to run the risk of being killed. But if I fall, I'll fall five feet four inches forward in the fight for freedom." How shall we understand these kinds of people? It is not simply that they were extraordinary; they were persons who understood that they had a gift for a moment, a gift for their moment in the course of human history.

I will leave you alone in just a moment, Mr. Obama, but before I do, let me tell you something that you may not have realized. There may be a few people in Washington, DC, and a few more across this country, and a few more in places around the world that have opinions and perspectives different from yours. Moreover, they may at times seek to voice those differences vociferously. Like everyone else gathered here, the humanness of your nature means that sometimes it will not be easy to hear or deflect these comments and criticisms. When it seems like it's getting next to you, I advise you to do two important things. First, look to your wife, your life-companion for support and encouragement. Second, and most important, remember the words of Mordecai saying to *you* that "perhaps, just perhaps, you are where you are for such a time as this." Understand, Mr. Obama, that God has prepared you, God has placed you, and God will not forsake you.

Remember the God you serve and what God has done in the past for others who were called into service. Ruth was deserted and abandoned, but God had a purpose for her. Rahab was a woman of ill repute, but God had a purpose for her. Jacob was a reformed liar, but God had a purpose for him. David was the runt of the litter, but God had a purpose for him. Moses was a former fugitive from justice, but God had a purpose for him. Daniel found himself surrounded by carnivores, but God had a purpose for him. Saul of Tarsus breathed murderous threats upon the children of God, but God had a purpose for him. Yes, the best news is the Good News; God had a purpose when God prepared redemption in the person of Jesus Christ and placed him at the nexus of human pain and suffering. It was done so that our burden could be lifted for such a time as this.

If God is in the transformation business, which God is; if God is in the redemption business, which God is; and if God is in the salvation business, which God is; then it is clear that God has a purpose for you, Mr. Obama, and for all of us as well for such a time as this. And here is some assurance we all can carry with us as we go to the places God has prepared us and placed us:

> Just when I need Him, He is my all, Answering when upon Him I call; Tenderly watching lest I should fall, Just when I need Him most.[2]

NOTES

1. President-elect Obama and his family were present at Nineteenth St. Baptist Church when this sermon was preached on January 18, 2009.

2. William C. Pool, "Just When I Need Him Most," 1907.

the audacity of faith

ABOUT THE CONTRIBUTORS

Melvin Bray is founder and director of the missional youth development nonprofit *Kid Cultivators* (kidcultivators.org). He teaches at Pine Forge Academy, a historically African American Seventh-day Adventist boarding school in northeastern Pennsylvania.

Brad R. Braxton, M.Div., Ph.D., is senior minister of the Riverside Church in New York City. Formerly on faculty at Wake Forest and Vanderbilt, he was a Rhodes Scholar at the University of Oxford. He has written widely on the interface between New Testament studies and preaching.

Valerie Bridgeman, M.Div., Ph.D., teaches Hebrew Bible, homiletics, and worship at Memphis Theological Seminary. She is founding director of the school's Return Beat Theology and Arts Institute. She served as coeditor of *Those Preaching Women: A Multicultural Collection* and *Africana Worship Book*, Years B and C.

Leslie D. Callahan, M.Div., Ph.D., is assistant professor of modern church history and African American religion at New York Theological Seminary in New York City. She previously taught at the University of Pennsylvania in Philadelphia. She regularly comments on current events on both religion and public policy on her blog, What Callahan Thinks.

Tony Campolo, Ph.D., is a prolific author, popular speaker, and professor emeritus of sociology at Eastern University. For ten years he was on the faculty of the University of Pennsylvania. He is founder and president of the Evangelical Association for the Promotion of Education (EAPE). He has authored thirty-five books.

Luis Cortés Jr., M.S., M.Div., D.D., is founder and president of Esperanza, a national network of more than 12,000 Hispanic community and faith-based organizations, based in Philadelphia, Pennsylvania. With a graduate degree in economic development, this ordained American Baptist minister was named by *TIME* magazine as one of "25 Most Influential Evangelicals" in 2005.

Curtiss Paul DeYoung, M.Div., Ed.D., is professor of reconciliation studies at Bethel University in St. Paul, Minnesota. Ordained in the Church of God (Anderson, Indiana), he has served in urban ministry settings and multiracial congregations. He is author of several books, including *Reconciliation* and *Coming Together* (Judson Press) and *Living Faith*.

Valerie Elverton Dixon, Ph.D., is an independent scholar and founder of JustPeaceTheory.com. In addition to the lectures and essays posted on her own site, her writings can be found on sojo.net and beliefnet.net. She has taught Christian ethics at United Theological Seminary in Dayton, Ohio, and at Andover Newton Theological School in Newton Centre, Massachusetts.

Ken Fong, M.Div., D.Min., is senior pastor of Evergreen Baptist Church of Los Angeles, located in Rosemead, California. A noted conference speaker and church leader, he is a pioneer in multi-Asian and multiethnic church ministry. His is author of *Pursuing the Pearl: A Comprehensive Resource for Multi-Asian Ministry* (Judson Press) and *Secure in God's Embrace*.

Wil Gafney, Ph.D., is associate professor of Hebrew and Hebrew Scripture at the Lutheran Theological Seminary in Philadelphia and an Episcopal priest serving as an associate at the African Episcopal Church of St. Thomas in Philadelphia. She is author of *Daughters of Miriam: Women Prophets in Ancient Israel*.

Derrick Harkins, M.Div., D.Min., is senior pastor of Nineteenth Street Baptist Church in Washington, DC, where the Obamas are now members. He previously served as pastor of New Hope Baptist Church in Dallas. He regularly leads mission teams to the Caribbean and has also led a team to Rwanda.

James Henry Harris, M.Div., Ph.D., is senior pastor of Second Baptist Church of Richmond, Virginia, and professor of pastoral theology and homiletics at the Samuel Dewitt Proctor School of Theology at Virginia Union University in Richmond. He has written widely on homiletics and pastoral theology.

Dwight M. Hopkins, M.Div., Ph.D., is professor of theology at the University of Chicago Divinity School and an ordained minister in the ABCUSA. He serves as senior editor of the Henry McNeil Turner/Sojourner Truth Series in Black Religion (Orbis). A frequent commentator on CNN and National Public Radio, he has written widely on black and liberation theology.

Carolyn Ann Knight, M.Div., D.Min., is former homiletics professor in New York City and Atlanta. She is presently president and founder of Carolyn Ann Knight/Can Do! Ministries, Inc., a preventive advocacy ministry that seeks to motivate youth and young adults. She is contributor to the *Those Preaching Women* series (Judson Press) and to *The African American Pulpit*.

Joseph R. Kutter, M.Div, D.Min., is acting executive director of the American Baptist Ministers Council. In his thirty-nine years as an ordained ABC minister, he has served as pastor of five congregations, most recently as senior pastor of First Baptist Church of Topeka, Kansas. Previously, he was also a trustee of Colgate Rochester Crozer Divinity School.

Marvin A. McMickle, D.Min., Ph.D., is senior pastor at Antioch Baptist Church in Cleveland, Ohio, and professor of homiletics at Ashland Theological Seminary in Ohio. Author of a dozen books, he worked on *The Audacity of Faith* while serving as visiting professor of homiletics at Yale Divinity School. He was an Obama delegate to the 2008 Democratic National Convention.

A. Roy Medley, M.Div., is general secretary of American Baptist Churches USA. As the chief executive officer of the 1.5 million-member denomination since 2002, he exercises executive and prophetic initiative in support of an effective mission outreach for ABCUSA. Previously he served as executive minister for American Baptist Churches of New Jersey.

Otis Moss Jr., M.Div., D.Min., is pastor emeritus of Olivet Institutional Baptist Church in Cleveland, Ohio. He delivered the Lyman Beecher Lectures on Preaching at Yale University. *Ebony* magazine twice named him one of the nation's top fifteen black preachers. The *New York Times* named him as one of Barack Obama's five spiritual advisers.

Otis Moss III, M.Div., is senior pastor of Trinity United Church of Christ in Chicago, the congregation where the Obamas were formerly members. Author of *Redemption in a Red Light District* and coauthor of *The Gospel Remix: Reaching the Hip Hop Generation*, he has also contributed to *The African American Pulpit*, *Sojourners*, and *Urban Spectrum*.

William H. Myers, D.Min., Ph.D., is professor of New Testament and director of the Black Church Studies program at Ashland Theological Seminary in Ohio, and pastor of New Mt. Zion Baptist Church in Cleveland. An expert on African American call stories, he is also author of *The Irresistible Urge to Preach* and *God's Yes Was Louder Than My No.*

Anthony B. Pinn, Ph.D., is the Agnes Cullen Arnold Professor of Humanities and professor of religious studies at Rice University in Houston, Texas. He is executive director of the Society for the Study of Black Religion and founding director of Houston Enriches Rice Education (HERE). He is author or editor of eighteen books on various aspects of African American religion.

Chris Rice, M.Div., is codirector of the Center for Reconciliation at Duke Divinity School. Previously he served seventeen years in reconciliation and justice ministries in Jackson, Mississippi. He is coauthor of *Reconciling All Things* (with his Duke colleague, Emmanuel Katongole) and *More Than Equals* (with Spencer Perkins), and author of *Grace Matters*.

J. Alfred Smith Sr., M.Div, D.Min., is a well-known author, respected professor, and pastor emeritus of Allen Temple Baptist Church in Oakland, California. He is a past president of American Baptist Churches of the West and the Progressive National Baptist Convention, Inc.

Mitzi J. Smith, M.Div., Ph.D., is assistant professor of New Testament and early Christianity at Ashland Theological Seminary's campus in Detroit. She is an ordained itinerant elder in the African Methodist Episcopal Church. Dr. Smith was also a contributor to *True to Our Native Land: An African American New Testament Commentary*.

Robin L. Smith, M.Div., Ph.D., is an ordained ABCUSA minister, licensed psychologist, national television personality, and popular keynote speaker. Perhaps best known for her appearances on *The Oprah Winfrey Show*, Dr. Smith's relationship book, *Lies at the Altar: The Truth about Great Marriages*, is a national best seller.

Gina M. Stewart, M.Div., D.Min., serves as pastor of Christ Missionary Baptist Church in Memphis, Tennessee. She was the first female to be elected as pastor of a Baptist church in Memphis. She serves as an advisory board member for *The African American Pulpit*, and she was a contributor to the *African American Devotional Bible* (Zondervan).

Leonard Sweet, M.Div., Ph.D., is the E. Stanley Jones Professor of Evangelism at Drew University in Madison, New Jersey, where he has also served as vice president of academic affairs and dean of the School of Theology. He previously served as president of United Theological Seminary in Dayton, Ohio. He is author of dozens of books and hundreds of articles.

Gardner C. Taylor, M.Div., D.D., is pastor emeritus of Concord Baptist Church in Brooklyn, New York. A past president of the Progressive National Baptist Convention, he delivered the Lyman Beecher Lectures on Preaching at Yale University. President Bill Clinton awarded him the Presidential Medal of Freedom. *Time* magazine named him "Dean of America's Black Preachers."

Emilie M. Townes, M.Div., Ph.D., is an ordained ABCUSA clergy serving as associate dean of academic affairs and the Andrew W. Mellon Professor of African American Religion and Theology at Yale Divinity School. In 2008 she was elected president of the American Academy of Religion. She has written widely on issues of ethics and womanist ethics.

Harold Dean Trulear, M.Div., Ph.D., is associate professor of applied theology at Howard University School of Divinity in Washington, DC, and president of GLOBE Community Ministries in Philadelphia. A fellow at the Center for Public Justice, he serves as a consultant to the Annie E. Casey Foundation in their work on religion and prisoner reentry.

Raphael G. Warnock, M.Div., Ph.D., serves as the fifth senior pastor of the Historic Ebenezer Baptist Church of Atlanta, spiritual home of Rev. Dr. Martin Luther King Jr. Known for his local activism and global vision, he is sought after as a scholar and a preacher.

William H. Willimon, M.Div., S.T.D., is bishop of the United Methodist Church of Northern Alabama and adjunct professor at Duke University Divinity School where he previously served for twenty years as dean of chapel and professor of Christian ministry. Recipient of numerous honorary degrees, he is author of nearly sixty books.

Philip Yancey is an award-winning author and one of the most popular speakers in evangelical Christian circles today. With graduate degrees in English and communications, he serves as editor-at-large for *Christianity Today* and *Books and Culture*. His more than twenty books include best-selling titles *The Jesus I Never Knew* and *What's So Amazing about Grace?*